"Chris Brown's story is one of disappointment, poverty, heartbreak, and pain. But through it all, he found hope and restoration in Jesus and is living proof that your past doesn't define who you can become. If you or someone you know has lost hope, this book has the power to help you become restored."

Craig Groeschel, pastor of Life.Church
and *New York Times* bestselling author

"Telling our story gives others permission to enter and read the pages of our heart. Chris Brown has done exactly that. From his acknowledgments to his afterword, not only will you be welcomed in like a trusted friend; you will be stirred toward possible change in the hurtful places of your own history. *Restored* is full of healing insights and hopeful instructions. Wrap up in this vulnerable offering and experience God at work."

Patsy Clairmont, speaker, author, and coach

"None of us get to choose what kind of upbringing we'll have, but we do get to choose what we do with it. Chris chose to face his painful past and allow God to restore what was broken. This isn't just an encouraging example; this is hope for us all!"

Dave Ramsey, bestselling author and radio host

"There is no gold in pain and trauma, but there is something in our pain and trauma that can be turned into gold. Chris Brown gets this concept. If you have pain in your past, you'll find a guide to redeem that pain in this book."

Donald Miller, bestselling author of *Building a StoryBrand*
and CEO of StoryBrand

"I have watched Chris's inspiring ministry journey for years and have always appreciated how he connects with others with genuine authenticity and wisdom while also faithfully leading his family with love and integrity. I continue to be touched by his eternal perspective about all the unfortunate and even tragic events from his past. There is no doubt that *Restored* will not only inspire you but also equip and encourage you."

Darryl Strawberry, evangelist and four-time
World Series champion

"Chris Brown had my attention with the title of this book! Restoration is a desire of every human being on the planet (well, the ones who are honest!). Restoration to Jesus and others is the only path to peace worth pursuing. And while a lot of people may say this is true, Chris doesn't just dive into theological and philosophical rabbit holes but rather, through storytelling and biblical application, shows practical ways for anyone (no matter where they are in their spiritual journey) to begin their journey to restoration."

Perry Noble, senior pastor at Second Chance Church

"Chris's vulnerability in sharing his story, and the lessons learned from it, paint an amazing picture of how God can breathe hope into any situation. Chris's approach looks beyond the pain of his past to the hope and victory in Jesus and encourages us to do the same."

J. Todd Mullins, senior pastor at Christ Fellowship Church

"This book is more than a compilation of pages filled with information; it's actually a blueprint for transformation. Chris masterfully uses parts of his life as a picture of possibility for ours. He shows us that although there may be seasons when our life seems to be in ruins, it doesn't have to ruin us. Why settle for ruins when we can be restored?"

Dr. Dharius Daniels, lead pastor at Change Church
and author of *Relational Intelligence*

Restored

Restored

TRANSFORMING THE STING OF YOUR

PAST INTO PURPOSE FOR TODAY

Chris Brown

Revell

a division of Baker Publishing Group
Grand Rapids, Michigan

Published by Revell
a division of Baker Publishing Group
PO Box 6287, Grand Rapids, MI 49516-6287
www.revellbooks.com

Printed in the United States of America

Library of Congress Cataloging-in-Publication Data
Names: Brown, Chris, 1977– author.
Title: Restored : transforming the sting of your past into purpose for today / Chris Brown.
Description: Grand Rapids, MI : Revell, a division of Baker Publishing Group, 2022.
Identifiers: LCCN 2021035556 | ISBN 9780800740436 (cloth) | ISBN 9781493434404 (ebook)
Subjects: LCSH: Self-actualization (Psychology)—Religious aspects—Christianity. | Regret—Religious aspects—Christianity.
Classification: LCC BV4598.2 .B765 2022 | DDC 248.4—dc23
LC record available at https://lccn.loc.gov/2021035556

Some of the names and details of the people and situations described in this book have been changed or presented in composite form in order to ensure the privacy of those involved.

Published in association with The Bindery Agency, www.TheBinderyAgency.com.

Baker Publishing Group publications use paper produced from sustainable forestry practices and post-consumer waste whenever possible.

22 23 24 25 26 27 28   7 6 5 4 3 2 1

Contents

Contents

Acknowledgments

First and foremost, I am thankful to God. I am eternally grateful for your grace, your protection, your guidance, and your trust in me to steward so much opportunity for your glory. This life is a supernatural gift from you that I am resolved not to get too familiar with or accustomed to. Thank you, Lord.

Holly Christine Brown, I'm incredibly grateful that you took a risk on the mysterious college kid with the sketchy past. I know there is real-life baggage that comes with a story like mine, and you have been so patient and graceful. You truly are a Proverbs 31 wife. And a deep heartfelt thank you for your help on this book project. Your writing gift and your ability to mine deep into my guarded heart for the raw emotion are gifts that I pray people will get to enjoy for years to come. There is nobody on this planet who has developed the depth of my faith like you have, and I couldn't imagine doing life with anyone else.

Patricia Ann Brown, I know you did the best you could. At the end of the day, you stayed. You fought the fight. Your kids are thriving now, and despite all the pain, we know deep down that you loved us the best you knew how to. We still love you deeply. You will always be Mom, and we look forward to being reunited someday when we're worshiping the King together . . . forever.

And all the pastors, coaches, leaders, and teachers, there were some major gaps in my life that desperately needed to be filled. Thank you so much for not only filling those gaps but also going above and beyond to love me and to speak life into me throughout the years. Don't for one second ever doubt the impact you are having. Each of you impacted me in a very significant way. I brag about each of you often, and God and I have very intentional conversations about how to steward all the deposits you have made in my life for decades.

1

An Invitation

There I was, sitting in the boardroom with my boss, my boss's boss, and several of my colleagues as they reviewed my most recent speech to thousands of people. The speech was titled "Stewardship Changes Everything." It was about how to handle money. Don't freak out or throw this book aside; I promise this is not a money management book. My wife, Holly, tells me I have spent far too much time teaching about money when it can all be summed up in these five words: spend less than you make. She says, "We get it. We get it." Understanding this is not the problem; the problem is none of us want to do it.

But that's not the point here today. The point is, I was sitting at the big oak boardroom table having to watch myself on camera, which is agonizing enough, but having to watch yourself in front of your bosses and peers is pure agony. I like to think it's especially agonizing for me because, truthfully, I don't like speaking. I know I am not good at it. I never sought to do this with my life. If I could stay behind the scenes and let the big personalities take the stage instead of me, now that would be a dream come true. But somehow, I ended up here . . . in a boardroom as my bosses and my peers frame-by-frame critiqued my public speaking ability.

As my speech came to a close and I began to walk off-screen, my boss shut off the video and we all sat there fluctuating between staring at each other and staring at the screen in an effort to appear deep in thought about the performance. We all knew what was really happening. Every one of us was wondering who was going to give me the first blow below the belt. I began to sweat—that awful, nervous sweat that smells much different than a hard workout sweat. I *hate* this part of the process. I am already insecure about my speaking ability, and I really don't enjoy people I admire telling me exactly how I fell short. But I'm a big boy, and there is no getting out of this at our organization, so I'm just going to sit here, keep on with my nervous sweating, and take it like a man.

There were many constructive criticisms spoken in the next few minutes, but I remember only one. Someone I deeply admire looked at me and said, "Chris, you have to learn to be more vulnerable onstage. All we see is this good-looking, all-American man born with a silver spoon in his mouth and who now has his own all-American family. People can't relate to that. Your opportunities to this point appear to have been endless. You've had to have had a better life than most."

I sat there in stunned silence. Do I even begin to tell him how *incredibly wrong* this assumption is, or do I just politely smile and nod? I've spent the majority of my adult life hiding the disastrous trauma that I came from, and now he's telling me I come across as too privileged. In some ways, I felt accomplished in the most successful moment of my life. I had done it. I had fooled them all. A satisfaction rushed over me that people thought I actually came from something. They assumed that I had a good upbringing, the kind that would make the average person jealous.

And yet, in that part of me that houses me and only me, the part of me that I try not to pay attention to but it nags at me like a toddler wanting a pack of fruit snacks, I felt like a phony. A lie. I had arrived, except . . . it wasn't really me. It was a version of me that I had spent my entire adult life creating. And that version had made it. But the real person I was, the real Chris Brown, that person, if you knew him, you would never have him sitting in this boardroom. He never would have turned your head. He wouldn't be here because he wouldn't have made it.

My boss's boss saw an all-American boy, and I see a boy more familiar with the homeless shelters across our country than the arenas. He saw good looks; I see forgotten. He saw a silver spoon; I see poverty. He saw opportunity; I see survival. While I sat there and listened to him, I couldn't help but wonder if I had finally made it or if I had just committed the worst possible crime against myself. I was too embarrassed to admit who I was and where I was from, that I had created a version of myself for the world to see. And now my boss was telling me he wanted to see the real me. This would be the most courageous work in my life to date. I reluctantly opened up and began to tell him and the rest of the people in the room my story. My real story.

My story isn't pretty, but I deeply care for most of those who played a part in it. As with any story, there are good parts and bad parts, sometimes even played by the same person. And it's this contradiction of being both provider and abuser or caretaker and addict that makes it so hard for me to know where my own emotions lie when it comes to parts of my story. So, because I was confused internally and did not want to dishonor the people who I believe were doing the best they knew how, I rarely shared my story and I've never put pen to paper. But in the last decade, those key players who left me conflicted all passed away. And through the hard work of grieving their loss and healing from wounds we endured together, I began to understand the roles they played, God's redemption of it all, and the restoration that can be found in the sting of our deepest pain.

As I sat in that boardroom telling chapter after chapter of my story, I kept thinking, *While I was surviving my childhood, God was building something in me so that I could do much more on this earth than just survive.* I'm not alone in this. In the Old Testament of the Bible, while Moses was escaping the consequences of murdering someone, God was simultaneously making a leader. While Jonah was running away in fear, God was making him into a prophet. In the New Testament, while Peter was hanging his head in shame over his disloyalty, at the same time, Jesus was appointing him a leader of his church. God just does that.

While we think we are merely surviving our pain, God is pioneering something new in us. Something useful for this world. Something beautiful. Sometimes the best thing we can do when going through pain is merely go through it and leave the rest with God. Going through pain is harder work than we think. It physically and emotionally exhausts us. It makes simple tasks like getting out of bed or taking a shower feel like a mountain to climb before our day even starts. And the tempting thing about pain is that we don't have to feel it if we don't want to. In today's world, we don't have to go through pain if we choose not to. We have so many options to numb ourselves and skirt around it. We can take the sleeping pills, drink the drink, scroll the screen, or drown ourselves in activity. We don't have to feel pain if we choose not to.

I understand that many of you reading this book may not practice the same faith in Jesus that I do, and I respect that. But I believe that if you keep reading with me, you will see that the message of this book will prove to be helpful and healing to you regardless of your faith.

> While we think we are merely surviving our pain, God is pioneering something new in us. Something useful for this world. Something beautiful.

I think together we will find common ground in the trauma we have endured. We can celebrate the parts of us that we have been able to pick up and how we have moved on despite what we've been through. And I believe the parts of us that are still broken will find healing as we process our pain.

I want to share with you something I learned from Jesus's life that I think is very important for us in the most painful moments of our lives. The night before his death, Jesus was in what many would consider the most emotionally painful night of his life. He knew what was coming, that in a matter of hours he would be betrayed by one closest to him, beaten almost to death, mocked by those he thought loved him, rejected by his best friend, and ultimately killed by public crucifixion. Complete shame, humiliation, and physical pain were just around the corner. Jesus knew this moment was coming, and he was in emotional torment. He asked his best friends to walk with him to a quiet garden flourishing with olive trees where he could pray. When they arrived at this garden, Jesus turned to his friends and basically explained, "Hey, guys, I'm going to need a minute to myself. Will you stay here and pray for me while I go and pray alone? My anxiety is out of control, and I need to pray alone."

Jesus then walked away to pray to his Father, but "when he rose from prayer and went back to the disciples, he found them asleep, exhausted from sorrow" (Luke 22:45). The disciples were sleeping, not praying. But look at this: they were sleeping because they were *exhausted from sorrow*. They were grieving. Jesus had told them he was about to die. His predictions had a 100 percent success rate. Jesus was not only their leader but also one of their closest friends, and he was in deep anguish. The disciples were feeling that pain of grief . . . you know, the pain that makes your chest physically ache, your head throb, your muscles tense up. The pain that forms a lump in your throat. The kind of pain that begs you to close your eyes and escape it. That's the pain they were in, and they just wanted it to go away, so they did what they knew to do. They fell asleep. They didn't have all the numbing options we have today, so they numbed their pain the best way they knew how . . . by falling asleep.

The pain of this life can get to be too much. Too hard. Too overwhelming. The shame all-consuming. The grief deafening. The fear paralyzing. And the temptation when the pain is too much to bear? To fall asleep. To numb ourselves to this life. Some of us with sleep, but others with alcohol, sex, Netflix, social media, or drugs.

And this, my friend, is when we become a casualty, not a casualty to death but a casualty to life.

I have felt this temptation for most of my life. The pain of my life was too much. I wanted to shut down. I preferred being a dead man walking over feeling the pain. And we all know what this looks like: Our hearts keep beating but we quit living. We share the same bed with our spouse, but there's no intimacy. We spend time with our kids, but our hearts never smile at their playfulness. Our bodies show up at the party, but our minds are trapped in a world far, far away. We have become a casualty . . . to life.

And here is the tragedy of falling asleep to life: yes, we do not feel the pain, but we also forfeit the ability to feel the joy that life cradles. You see, you can't have joy without pain. They flow together. When we become a casualty to life, we miss the joy of our spouse's affection, the innocence in a child's giggle, the celebration of a home run in the ninth inning, the simple pleasure found in a cup of coffee or a beautiful sunset, the satisfaction of opening a new tube of toothpaste, or the awe of noticing a sky full of stars. When we choose not to feel pain, we also choose to miss life.

Have you found yourself here? Some thing, some pain not only took your past but is also stealing your present. It's tempting you day after day to pick up the bottle, to sleep, to take the pills, to keep scrolling. Maybe it's the rejection of a spouse, the grief from losing a loved one, the abuse you endured, the failure you caused, the hopelessness of feeling stuck. Do you fight the urge to quit living in order to escape the pain?

In Luke 22:41–44, Jesus shows us a better way to cope with our pain:

> He withdrew about a stone's throw beyond them, knelt down and prayed, "Father, if you are willing, take this cup from

me; yet not my will, but yours be done." An angel from
heaven appeared to him and strengthened him. And being
in anguish, he prayed more earnestly, and his sweat was like
drops of blood falling to the ground.

Jesus *went through* his pain. The emotional pain in the
garden almost killed him, but he went through it. He pushed
through the anguish. He sat with it. He gave space to his
pain. He put words to what he was enduring, and he offered
those words to his Father. Jesus felt the pain, and he didn't
quit. He stayed awake to this life. He showed up.

And look what happened because of it. God sent angels
in the moment of his greatest pain to strengthen him. Like
there was with Jesus, there is great strength awaiting us if
we choose to *go through* the pain.

There is life to be had on the other side of our pain. And
more than just strength, there are great gifts waiting for us,
gifts that the pain we barely survived has brought us, gifts
that will make this life something to smile at again. Something to look at in wonder again. Something to enjoy living
in again. No matter what you have endured, your life is worth
showing up for. Pain is worth traveling through because of
what we find on the other side.

So let's do this together. Let's wake up, go through the
pain, and enjoy the beauty of awakening to life on the other
side. Let's be overcomers, not of death but of life.

Accused, oppressed, bound up, hungry, homeless, impov-
erished, in desperate need of help, wounded, troubled—all
of these words described me at some point in my life. Would
they describe you at some point in your life? Are you living
under financial stress like never before? Are you chained to
an addiction? Do you feel enslaved to your boss? Is your soul

troubled day in and day out? Do the wounds of your past still haunt you? If you live with any one of these descriptors long enough, you will develop some scars.

My pain would still have bled, but I didn't let it. I spent decades running from it, trying to prove that those things never even bothered me. That was my numbing. I just didn't give it a lick of attention. I didn't acknowledge how much hurt I was in. How much

> No matter what you have endured, your life is worth showing up for. Pain is worth traveling through because of what we find on the other side.

insecurity from my past overwhelmed me in almost every setting I found myself in. It affected my marriage, my parenting, my job. I ran from it all until it would cause me to explode at my wife or kids for the smallest things. A few times when I was forced to face it in my job, I ran. I quit and moved on to the next thing. It was easier to start over than face the pain I had buried so deep.

I believe God is going to do something with our pain. Maybe you're like me and your past pain still oozes into your daily life and relationships. That very pain, when you not only survive it but also process it and heal from it, is what God will use to sculpt you into the most beautiful version of yourself. A version of you that is softer and more tender, that feels deeper, that empathizes with others in their pain. Your pain doesn't have to ruin you; rather, it can carry you right into your life's purpose. You see, pain recognizes pain.

A lonely person will notice the girl at the party in the corner by herself with her eyes down because they themselves have been lonely. The one who's been emptied because of addiction will notice the hollowness in another's eyes despite the makeup attempt to cover it. The anxious will notice the fidgety fingers and overtalking of another wrought with anxiety. We recognize in others the pain we ourselves have endured. When we see that pain and we remember what it felt like to be there—to want to hide in the corner at the party or to binge on alcohol to numb the anxiety—we will be compelled to step in and show compassion or offer a helping hand. When we do these things for others, we will be, as Isaiah said, "like a well-watered garden, like an ever-flowing spring" (Isa. 58:11 NLT). This is when we will begin to be known as "a rebuilder of walls and a restorer of homes" (Isa. 58:12 NLT). This is when our deepest pain will become our greatest beauty.

It all starts with going through our own pain. Allowing God to put a healing balm on the pain that still oozes. Letting that pain once and for all become a scar, a scar that reminds us why we stop to aid the lonely woman we see at the store or the drunk on the street corner, why we choose not to throw shade and instead offer compassion. I'm beginning to be okay with showing the world some of my scars. As you read about some of my scars in this book, my goal is that you will (1) see a path to heal from your wounds, and (2) begin to see your scars as something that can have purpose today.

Scars do not have to be the enemy's final blow that renders you useless. They can be the opposite of that. They can be something that drives you right into your life's greatest purpose.

Before we continue, I think it is important to note that I am not a licensed counselor. I'm just a man who, like you, has been through some things. But I hope my story will encourage you, inspire you, and also give you some very practical advice for your journey. This is my prayer for you:

Heavenly Father, I ask that you will ready the reader's heart to hear. I pray that you will speak directly to their heart and life. I pray that any hardness in their life that feels like protection will crumble at your feet. I pray that rejection will start to feel like acceptance and regrets will turn to freedom. Lord, show them you are a loving Father who is madly in love with them. Amen.

2

Past Heartache, Present Empathy

I was just a little over a year old when my biological father and my mom divorced. The only reason I was ever given for the divorce came from my father. He told me once when I was a teenager, "I left your mom because she couldn't sit still. She was always putzing around the house, cleaning this or organizing that, and I was like, 'Dang, woman. Sit down.' She never listened. She never would hold still and relax, so I left her."

I have been married for more than twenty years now, and would you hate me if I told you I honestly believed for the first decade of my marriage that my dad's explanation was a legit reason to leave someone? I may have even used it against my own wife a time or two. I know, it's ridiculous, and I'm not winning you over by admitting this. I definitely forfeit the husband of the year award for that one, but, honestly, that's what I was told and that's what I believed, until my wife challenged me on believing that bull. So, yes, I'm sure there were more "adult" reasons for their divorce, but I never knew them.

Regardless, I was a year old, and it was me, Mom, and a couple of pennies to our name from then on. We lived in Littleton, Colorado, and by the time I was about two, my mom had met another man. Even at a young age, I could tell this man was a drunk. And when he drank, he got angry, and my mom bore the brunt of his anger. Night after night, from the age of two until ten, I went to bed hearing my mom being belittled and thrown around. With this second relationship of my mom's, we inherited two older children in the home as well. I don't know why I was exempt from the abuse and the other kids were not, but for some reason, this man never touched me in an abusive way. You would think the new child would be the one being hurt the most, but for unknown reasons, I was protected the most. I do pride myself on the fact that my earliest memories are of me mastering the art of staying out of an angry drunk's line of vision.

Many times the abuse got to be too much for my mom. We followed the same cycle that it seems most women in abusive situations follow. My mom would tell me that a man should never hurt a woman like he was hurting her, so we were leaving. She was putting her foot down and would *never* allow this to happen again. I was so relieved every time she told me this because although he never did abuse me, I didn't know at the time that he was not *going to* abuse me. He hit the others often, and I always thought my turn was coming. As soon as I would hear him stumbling around the house and yelling, I thought for sure when he finished with Mom or his boys he'd find me and beat me. I was scared all the time in that house with him.

Time and time again, we would escape to a women's shelter and stay there as long as they would allow, which seemed like a couple of weeks to a month. I don't remember much about my time in those shelters except that I loved that there were no men. It was just moms and kids, and we had so much fun together, mostly because we didn't have to tiptoe around angry drunk men or try to find places to hide where they couldn't see us. We just got to run around and play with toy cars as much as we wanted.

When our time was up, no matter how determined my mom was *never* to go back, when the reality of being penniless with no place to lie down at night hit her, my mom always went back. I remember a couple of times we stayed a few nights in our car after our time at the shelter ran out, but the crisp Colorado air and cramped car situation eventually wore down her determination to make it on our own. She caved, and we were forced to return to an angry, volatile home.

When I was eight, my mom had another baby, Joel. Joel had pale white skin and the reddest hair I'd ever seen. We didn't look a thing alike, but I loved trying to help Mom with him. I'm sure I wasn't much help, but I remember giving him a bottle here and there and keeping an eye on him while Mom fixed dinner or when Mom's boyfriend would take her into the bedroom to slap her around. Before long, things had gotten progressively worse, and we were scared constantly. But my mom's self-esteem was in shambles, so we didn't leave.

One day, soon after my little brother was born and while my mom was tied up with caring for him, I was playing with a friend. We were talking about the WWE (well, back then it was still WWF) action figures kids had at school and how much we wished we had a few too. We decided that we were going to go to the local drug store and steal some, and, while we were at it, we'd get a couple of toy guns as well. It was the dead of summer and over ninety degrees that day. As we were gathering the supplies we needed to pull off the drug store theft, I confidently put on my mom's boyfriend's puffy winter coat. Then I strode down the street with my buddy as we reviewed our plan one final time.

As soon as we entered the store, I headed straight for the toy aisle . . . in my huge puffy winter coat . . . in the dead of summer. I didn't bother to look around because I had been watching WWE for a while now, and I knew that if an adult came after me, I could probably outrun them, but even if I couldn't, I had the Hulk Hogan leg drop down and I'd be out of the store before they knew what hit them. As I stuffed and stuffed, my friend kept frantically whispering, "Chris, stop. That's enough. We're going to get caught. Stop." Obviously, he had no idea how good I was at wrestling. I paid him no attention and kept stuffing. When I was satisfied with my collection, I headed straight for the exit.

Just as I was about to step outside, I felt a piercing pain on my right ear. It hurt so bad that I squealed and started walking backward in an effort to relieve the pain. The store manager was pulling me by my ear to his office. He reminded me in a rather gruff tone that the pain in my ear was nothing compared to the pain my parents would be giving me as soon as he called them. My mom retrieved me from his office about thirty minutes later and told me to stay in my room until her boyfriend returned home from work. I thought for sure I was going to get my first beating that day. Within an hour of consigning me to my room, my mom slung the door open and said with tears in her eyes, "Get in the car now." And out of crippling fear, we fled again and spent the next several days and nights hidden far from the house in my mom's car—a brown 1979 Dodge Diplomat. Mom would later tell me she saw a wrath in her boyfriend's eyes that day that she was determined to prevent me from seeing. But, even so, we eventually went back.

Even though my mom was scared of her boyfriend and fearful of being penniless without him, she did her best to make some great memories for my brother and me. I'll never forget my tenth birthday. I had been begging my mom for a dog for years, and the answer was always no. No because Joel is a handful already and a puppy would be as well. No because dogs are expensive. No because you aren't old enough to take responsibility for a dog and I have enough on my plate already. Although I asked my mom regularly, I had given up on the hope of getting my own dog. But on my big day, I was handed two presents, one that kept rattling and making noises and another very heavy box. I received a bag of dog food and a puppy named Ginger. I was completely shocked! Ginger was a golden cocker spaniel. She was the sweetest little thing, and her eyes told me that she just longed to obey and please me. She was small but mighty, and I was completely in love. I never cared even the least bit that she kept peeing all over the house.

I had begged for years, and finally I had a dog! Ginger and I spent all day together, and I took her everywhere with me. Mom took me to the pet store to get her a leash and collar. I picked a bright blue one. I'd put her leash on every morning, and she would play outside with me all day long during those final days of summer break. I relished having my own dog. Whenever Mom's boyfriend started beating my mom or his kids, I'd grab Ginger and we'd escape outside or, if it was past dark, into my bedroom, where we would play quietly together. Ginger was the best part of life in that house.

It wasn't but a couple of months after my tenth birthday that the boyfriend's drinking and obsession with controlling my mom escalated until it all came crashing down on one brisk fall night. He had been out drinking and probably using as well, but I was too young to differentiate high from drunk at the time. Regardless, he was in rare form even for his standards. He came home convinced my mom was leaving him, and he was bound and determined to stop her at any cost. He didn't even take time to park the car in the driveway. He literally drove his mideighties sedan *into* our living room. I remember Mom screaming that he was an idiot and could have killed one of us in his drunken rage, but he was in no mood for a lecture. He was in charge, and he let that be known right away.

He stumbled through the living room and down the hall, running his hands along the walls on either side to steady himself, and went right into Joel's nursery. He picked up my two-year-old brother and walked into the kitchen. We were all scared, and I wanted to run and hide in my room, but my mom was screaming, and he had my brother, so I had to see what he was doing. He grabbed a sharp knife from the utensil drawer. He took that knife in one hand and my baby brother in the other and proceeded to hold the knife to Joel's throat and scream at my mom in a slurred voice.

My mom just kept crying and begging him to calm down. She dropped to her knees and promised over and over that she would not leave. She assured him through her sobs that she loved him. I don't know exactly what happened next, but I remember the look in her boyfriend's eyes changed. I didn't know it at the time, but now I realize his eyes were wavering from rage to fear. Or maybe from hallucination to reality? He set Joel down and called 911 himself. He told the police that he was afraid of himself and what he might do to his family. When they started asking him questions, his eyes changed again, and that scared look went back to rage. He hung up the phone and immediately grabbed Joel from my mom's arms. With the knife in his hand, he kept barking at my mom and daring her to leave him while he paced through our demolished living room. This seemed like it went on forever, but I'm sure in reality it was just a few minutes. The next thing I knew, the police busted into the house through the back door in the kitchen, where my mom's boyfriend was now standing and ranting. In an instant, one officer pulled his hair straight back from behind while catching Joel, and another grabbed his hand with the knife. A third officer tackled him from behind. It was very impressive and a takedown I will never forget. He was cuffed and immediately taken to jail.

That night frightened my mom so much, and it was finally enough to seal the deal that we would not stay. Roof over our heads or not, we weren't staying at his house ever again. We didn't just have to leave the house; we had to leave Colorado. My mom had no idea how long he would be in jail, and she knew he'd come looking for her the moment he was released. Mom handed me a gym bag and told me to put in three of everything: my three favorite pants, shirts, underwear, and socks. She said when I was done doing that, I could pick one toy as long as it would fit in the bag with my clothes. I figured we were heading to the shelter again.

Once my mom was done talking to the police officers, she explained to me that one of the officers was going to give us a ride to the shelter. (We had only one car, and, well, that car and our TV stand were currently sharing the same space in our living room.) She told me with a big smile slapped over a tear-stained face that it would be a fun adventure to get to ride in a *real* police car. Maybe it was my fear still lingering from the night's events, but I wasn't convinced that anything about the rest of the night was going to be fun.

On the way to the shelter, Mom, Joel, Ginger, and I were all squeezed into the back of the police car. Mom explained to me that we were going to stay only a couple of days while our car was getting fixed, and then we were going on a trip to see my biological dad, who had moved to California a couple of years earlier. Now that sounded like a fun adventure! I hadn't talked to or seen my dad in years, and being with him was something I dreamed of often.

But then she broke the bad news to me. Mom said there was one really big problem with this entire scenario: Ginger. She wasn't allowed at the shelter, and Mom said she couldn't come with us on our trip to California. So only a couple of months after receiving the best gift ever, I knew I wasn't going to get to keep Ginger. I sobbed from the moment she explained this until we got to the shelter. I held on to Ginger as tight as I could without hurting her. All of a sudden, I went from okay to not okay. I felt so scared. Scared about what had just happened. Scared about what was next. Scared the most about what would happen to Ginger. She was the best part of my life, and now she couldn't come with me.

When we arrived and climbed out of the police car, Mom was holding Joel in her arms and I was holding Ginger. Mom knelt down and told me the police officer was going to take Ginger and that I needed to give her to him. Tears were streaming down my face, and my arms were reluctant to let go. The police officer bent down and promised me that he would take very good care of Ginger and that the moment we returned from seeing my dad, he would bring her back to me. I reluctantly handed Ginger over to the police officer. We stayed in the shelter long enough for Mom to get the car repaired, and then we headed for California. We never went back to Colorado. We never went back for Ginger.

That was the day I learned about loss. Unfair loss. Loss because of someone else's actions.

A few years ago, Holly, our three kids, and I moved to Tennessee from Florida. We had no family there. We knew no one. After only a few days of being there, Holly met a sweet friend at the kids' bus stop. This woman was a godsend to Holly in this new city of strangers. She often brought Holly Starbucks coffee she'd pick up on her way home from work. She brought her flowers if she knew Holly was having a rough week. Once my daughter, Annie, overheard Holly telling me on Valentine's Day, "Please don't buy me flowers. If you are going to spend money on me, I'd prefer you spend it on things that don't die in three days." It wasn't long until one day Holly's new friend brought a beautiful arrangement by the house and Annie told her, "My mom doesn't like flowers. She says they are a waste of money because they die. But she does like coffee. And she likes olives too." Holly was so embarrassed, but her friend and I got a kick out of it.

During this season, Holly had to leave for work in rush hour. She needed to leave the house exactly twenty minutes after she put the kids on the bus. Almost every day, Holly would come flying into the house about twenty-five minutes after the kids had gotten on the bus, grab her computer and makeup bag, and fly out the door. I knew she had stood at that corner chatting with her new bestie until the last possible moment. I knew she would be late to work again, but I also knew her heart was full.

This amazing woman had two children, and she and her husband worked together. From everything we could tell, things were great. Until they weren't. One day, out of the blue seemingly to us, she told us that her husband had left her and the kids. Her rent was due in just a couple of days, and she wasn't able to pay it. We didn't have the money to pay her rent, and even if we scraped up enough for one month, we knew we were just buying time. "What should we do?" Holly asked me one night.

Without really thinking about it, I said, "We should bring her and the kids to live with us."

"Okay, but you should know something," Holly said. "Her daughter, Emma, is a *huge* animal person, and she has lots and lots of animals and critters. I'm not even sure what they all are, but there are a lot of aquariums and cages and a dog. I know there is a dog." In that moment, all I could think of was Ginger. The night my world was turned upside down by a man's actions. The night I had to give away my dog to that police officer.

"Tell her to bring every single animal she has. That little girl's world was just turned upside down. We are not going to ask her to give up anything else."

As I watched that mom and little ten-year-old girl bring in cage after cage to our bonus room, all I could think was that you never really understand the purpose of a chapter in your life until you are in the next one. Sometimes you don't see God's fingerprints in the middle of the chaos of your life until you look back years later. Twenty-eight years later, I was beginning to understand a little more about my past. Losing Ginger hurt. It was a pain I had never known before that day, and I think it was more pain than most ten-year-olds experience. But it wasn't just about Ginger. It was about everything that handing my favorite thing in the entire world over to a stranger stood for: unfair loss, confusion, fear of the unknown.

When I saw the look in Emma's eyes, I knew that look! I knew I couldn't make her world better for her. Her father had left, and he wasn't coming back. I couldn't take that pain away. But I could keep pain from heaping on top of pain. She was not going to lose one animal or critter she so dearly loved. I would make sure of it. My past heartache had become my present empathy.

You never really understand the purpose of a chapter in your life until you are in the next one.

Maybe you are struggling with the pain of unfair loss. Maybe the loss came because of someone else's choices. Maybe you lost your family at the hands of a spouse who walked out. Maybe you lost your career at the hands of a coworker who lied about you. Maybe you lost a community of friends at the hands of someone whose insecurity caused them to gossip about you.

Here's what I've learned about trying to survive the pain that comes with unfair loss.

My first instinct is to want justice. I want the person to pay for what they did to me. I want them to feel pain over the pain they caused me. I believe this feeling is valid and completely normal, but the problem is that it doesn't serve me well. It doesn't help me heal and move on. What I try to do when these feelings flood my mind is intentionally pause and reflect on how much I have needed to be the recipient of grace myself. I may not be ready to forgive, but I can acknowledge that I have made my own fair share of mistakes.

I also want an apology. I want to hear them say they are sorry. I want them to realize the pain they caused me. I want them to find me and beg for my forgiveness. You know what I have found to be true more often than not with regard to forgiveness? I don't get to hear "I'm sorry" until I am at a point where I don't need it to be healthy. It seems to me that people apologize most often when I have given up hope that they ever will. When I have learned to be happy and healthy without their apology. I don't need it. And then, if and when it does come, it's like icing on the cake. A reminder that God was still working on that painful situation long after he helped me heal from it.

> Forgiveness is letting go of what is behind you and choosing to focus instead on the good things you have today.

I've also learned that forgiving others heals you, not them. Sometimes forgiveness simply means you are giving up the hope of hearing them say they are sorry; you are giving up the hope for a better past and the need for answers or explanations they never gave you. Forgiveness is letting go of what is behind you and choosing to focus instead on the good things you have today.

Finally, I have learned that when we choose to transform the sting of past heartache into empathy for today, we find not only tremendous healing but also life-changing purpose and fulfillment.

3

Broke and Busted

The night we arrived in Huntington Beach, California, from Colorado, we stayed in a hotel. It was the first time I can remember being in a hotel. I'm sure it was the cheapest hotel in town, but to me it seemed like the most luxurious place I'd ever stayed. We had the whole room and bathroom to ourselves. We could watch TV from our bed! I learned that night that home was not a place. Home was wherever it was just the three of us and no extra man. Just me, my baby brother, and my mom. And Mom was not drunk. That was home. That was my safe place. Those were our happiest moments. I felt safe and happy in that cheap hotel room as I fell asleep under the flowered polyester comforter.

The next day my mom called my father and explained the predicament we were in. She asked him for one thousand dollars in back child support so we could get an apartment. The check didn't come that day, so we stayed another night

in the hotel. The next day there was still no check. I guess
my mom was out of money, because on the third night, we
slept under the pier. I'd never slept under a pier before, but
since our car was full of our few belongings, that wasn't an
option. I had never been to a beach before, and this was far
from what I dreamed my first beach experience would be
like. I wonder now if, being new to California, my mom just
didn't know where the shelters were.

I remember lying under that pier still being so sad about
Ginger. Mom said this was just like camping out together.
She had even thought to bring pillows from the hotel for us.
We weren't the only people under the pier, but people didn't
speak to each other. We all just minded our own business.
We were away from violent men, so that made everything
just fine and safe for me.

I don't know when the check came, how many nights we
spent under the pier, or even how we were able to receive a
check without having an address, but I do distinctly remember reading the check. It had one thousand dollars written in
the amount box. I had never in my life seen a check that big.
I determined right then and there that my dad was rich and
that this new life was going to be pretty dang good because
I had a rich dad and he lived close by. I don't think my mom
ever told my dad we were staying under a pier. I remember
hearing them talk on a pay phone a couple of times. There
wasn't yelling or screaming like with her last boyfriend. I
didn't know my dad, but he seemed nice. I felt bad for Joel
because he had a bad dad and I had a rich one.

With one thousand dollars in hand, we went apartment
shopping. My mom found us the perfect place on the corner
of Edwards and Warner in Huntington Beach: Ocean Breeze
Villas. Mom didn't have a job, and we didn't have a single

piece of furniture. Over the next few months, we watched for neighbors moving in, and then Mom would send me to ask them if we could have their empty cardboard boxes. We used boxes for everything, but mostly for end tables, a dining table, and clothing storage. Over time we confiscated a few smoke-filled and mildewed pieces of furniture from local dumpsters or driveways on bulk trash day. I was beginning to realize that these were our best days . . . the days when no man was in the picture, when it was just Mom, me, and Joel.

Furniture or no furniture, staying under a pier or in an apartment, living on food stamps or food pantries, we always had fun as long as men stayed away from my mom. I even made a few friends at the new apartment. Our favorite thing to do was play mud football and then run and jump in the community pool. We did this all summer long. We also caught crawdads in a sewer ravine near us. I would take them to the bait shop and sell them for twenty-five cents. Some days I would make three or four bucks! And the best part about the bait shop? Well, it was right next to a baseball card shop. So I would take my crawdad earnings, buy myself a pack of baseball cards and a Beckett price guide, and then give my mom the leftover money. Life was good, and I had a deep sense that things were going to be okay.

It wasn't long before I realized my mom didn't have the same sense that things were going to be okay. I remember my eleventh birthday. I was sitting on the floor in our furniture-less apartment. Sure, things weren't perfect. We had little to no food and boxes for end tables, but we were making it work. The roaches weren't even a big deal anymore. Sure, there was no bounce house like I'd heard a couple of the rich kids at school talk about having on their birthday. In fact, there probably wouldn't be any presents to open this year, but at least we weren't going from shelter to shelter running from a boyfriend anymore. I was disappointed that Mom wasn't going to make me a cake, but my greatest disappointment that day came when I looked into our empty kitchen and saw nothing except my mom. There wasn't a coffee machine or a can opener on the counter. No dishes in the sink.

It was all empty, except for my mom, who was standing there leaning against the brown Formica countertop. My mom, the one who was doing whatever she could to protect and provide for my brother and me. The look in her eyes wasn't the look of tiredness a single mom who is working multiple jobs has. I knew that look. This one was different. This was a look of complete hopelessness. A look of having no way out. A look that says there is no space for birthday joy or silly jokes. I think that was the day hopelessness won and would continue to win.

I didn't know much as an eleven-year-old, but in that moment, watching hopelessness swallowing my mom made me angry. It didn't seem fair to me. My dad had left her on her own, and the next guy had abused her. These men had made things worse for her, and now here she was, completely hopeless. I decided right then and there that when I got big, I was going to have enough money to have a bounce house and a cake on my birthday. It's the day I made an agreement with myself that I would not be in her shoes when I was older. I was going to be rich.

And then I got big. In fact, shortly after my wife, Holly, and I had our first child, I left my steady albeit low-paying job and went into real estate. We had saved up a little nest egg to give me time to get things rolling in the right direction. Before long, things were going well. I was closing on houses and even doing some house flipping on the side. We flipped our first house and made an extra thirty thousand dollars in thirty days! That was and still is *a lot* of money for us. I caught the fever. I started flipping houses left and right, and before long, I had borrowed one million dollars from the bank to front my house-flipping business.

This was all good until the market crashed shortly after I borrowed all that money. Seemingly overnight, I owned several houses I couldn't sell, and I could rent them for only pennies on the dollar. Holly and I held on, just barely, for three years after the housing market crash in 2007, coming up with every extra penny we could to pay the daunting house payments. We downsized, Holly went back to work (with three toddlers by this point), and I picked up every side hustle I could to make money on the side, but finally after three years and a ton of stress, we had to face the fact that we couldn't hold on any longer. We had to declare bankruptcy.

I felt like a total failure as a husband, as a father . . . as a man. I will never forget the morning of my court hearing. I asked Holly not to come because I didn't want to put her through the humiliation caused by my failed business ventures. We fought like a great team to hold on and not get here, but now that we were here, I wanted to do this part alone and spare her the shame that I knew this day would hold. While Holly tried to insist on coming to court to support me, we did have three toddlers and she had a full-time job. Getting a free pass not to show up for something that was going to be emotionally exhausting was most likely a gift to her.

I remember getting ready in the master bathroom. I remember leaning over the much-too-low sink and splashing water on my face. I remember looking in the mirror. I recognized the look in my eyes. I had seen it before. I knew that look. A hollow look. Empty eyes. As I studied myself in the mirror, I saw that same hopeless look I had seen in my mom's eyes as she stood in that empty kitchen on my eleventh birthday. The look that had made me promise myself I would never end up like her. That I would be rich. Rich enough to have birthday parties with cakes and bounce houses. Rich enough to have food in the cupboards and furniture in my apartment. I had failed. I was right where she was. Broke and busted.

I felt hopeless that morning and didn't know a way out. I felt like there was nobody I could turn to. I had nothing. I was walking into a courtroom almost penniless and would certainly be leaving penniless. I had never done this before. I didn't know anyone who had done this before. Would they take the roof over our heads? Our cars? I was flying by the seat of my pants, but I knew there was a very real possibility that I could leave the courtroom with nothing. That I might even have to give up my car and embarrassingly call a friend to ask them to come pick me up. Physically sick with nerves and filled with hopelessness, I walked into that courtroom, sat down on one of the hard benches, and waited for my turn to be publicly shamed and humiliated.

I stepped in front of the judge when she called my name. She asked me a few questions. "How much money is in your bank accounts?"

"I only have one. And it has twenty-five dollars. Which is the minimum to keep it open," I managed to get out even though I had to shove my hands in my pockets because they were shaking so bad.

"How many cars do you have and how much do you owe on them?"

"We have two cars. One is paid for, and the other we owe about five thousand dollars on."

And then came the questions I feared she was going to ask. "Do you have any cash hidden anywhere else? In CDs? In an account in someone else's name?"

Everything in me wanted to lie and say, "No, ma'am." But I did have some cash. I had pulled the last bit of money we had out of the bank and hid it in my sock drawer. I debated for a few seconds, but I knew I couldn't live with myself if I lied, and under oath at that. I simply said, "Yes, ma'am."

"Yes?" Her question back to me held a tone of surprise.

Oh no, am I going to be arrested for this? My mind began to panic, but I replied, "Yes. I have $8,703.88 in the top drawer of my dresser."

She matter-of-factly responded, "Well, before I finalize this bankruptcy, I want you to go home, get that cash, and turn it in to the court."

With everything in me, I knew we were screwed. That money was for our next couple of house payments and car payments, and a little extra for food and necessities to hold us over until our next paychecks. But I did it anyway. I turned it in and came home that night with not a penny to our name.

Holly and I have been clawing our way back every day since that day. We are okay. We have handled our money God's way, and he has been more than good to us. God has blessed us with good jobs and three healthy kids. That is beauty in and of itself, but the most beautiful thing I learned was that I don't have to be financially secure to live a generous life. I can be generous *while* I am working my way out of my own financial debt. Hannah taught me this lesson.

> I don't have to be financially secure to live a generous life.

I met Hannah a few years ago when she was in the seventh grade. She lived in our neighborhood. I remember seeing her a couple of times playing in the neighborhood park that we could view from our kitchen window. In 2015, the park was the place to be for all fourth to seventh graders in their neon-colored Nike Elites and LeBron James high-tops. Then I noticed that Hannah began to linger around the park and would often make her way over to our house to jump on the trampoline or play video games with our kids. I was getting used to seeing Hannah often, but I realized I didn't know much about her.

One night as I was watching game one of the NBA Finals with my kids and Hannah, I asked her several questions. What came out of her precious mouth wrecked me. Hannah is one of nine kids. She told me that her parents aren't divorced but that her dad doesn't live with her anymore. I asked her why not. She replied in a broken voice, "Because he was killed in a car accident two months ago. He was hit by a drunk driver." My heart fell to the floor. I no longer cared how many points LeBron scored or if my kids took their nightly shower. All I could think was, *This precious girl is fatherless. In an instant, her world was shattered.*

As I sat there with my mouth gaping open, my boys fighting over LeBron versus Curry versus Jordan, and Hannah quietly wiping her tears, I knew God was telling me, "She is going to have some gaps in her life. Some of the same gaps you had when you were her age. No father. No money. Step in and fill the ones you can. Chris, you know firsthand that I am the Father to the fatherless. Can you show her this through your actions?" Over the next week, I realized God wasn't talking anything huge but rather an ounce more intentionality to swing by Hannah's on the way to the pool and invite her to join us, to offer her a ride to church with us on Sunday, to include her in a kickball game, to put an extra burger on the grill for her, to show patience by staying and watching one more trick on the trampoline followed by a heartfelt compliment.

That was the day I realized that my past pain doesn't have to help hundreds or thousands, but it could help one. That day I realized that God was asking me to show his love and care not just to those under our roof but to one more. We don't have to be completely out of debt and squared away financially to start helping one more. And giving doesn't always mean money either. What if we were generous includers? What if we were intentional about including *one more* in what we are going to do anyway?

> We don't have to be completely out of debt and squared away financially to start helping one more.

I remember some days when my kids would ask me after work to throw the football or jump on the trampoline. I was tired and would have quickly said, "No, not now," but then I would see Hannah waiting for my reply with a mountain of expectation in her eyes. I knew that unless I stepped up, Hannah would never have a grown man throw a football with her, or watch her do tricks on the trampoline, or tell her she is a great runner. This thought pushed me past my exhaustion and into the backyard night after night. Hannah made me a better father to my own kids in the process. Hannah taught me what true generosity looks like and why it is important no matter how much money I have to my name. Past pain, present empathy.

And just a little side note to my bankruptcy story. About eighteen months after that awful day in court, I received a check in the mail with a note from the trustee that simply said, "In my eighteen-year career as a bankruptcy trustee, I have never seen this happen, but the bankruptcy judge has asked that we return to you the following amount. She said to say, 'Thank you for your honesty.'" It was the total amount of cash I had turned in that day plus my attorney fees for the bankruptcy.

The Bible tells us that the earth and all it contains are the Lord's. It tells us that God owns cattle on a thousand hills. God is clearly in charge, but he's also our loving Father who provides. He was that kind of Father for me, but he's not just some genie in the sky overseeing things.

My childhood taught me what it was like to live below the poverty line, but it was my own choices and actions that bankrupted my family. It was the pain of sitting in that failure, that embarrassment, that gave me compassion for those who find themselves in the same situation. In fact, I give much of my time to helping individuals, churches, and businesses get out of debt and stay out of debt. My goal is to remember what the financial hopelessness felt like and to redeem it by letting it fuel me to help others battling the same emotions and situations.

You may be on the verge of financial ruin. But please hear me when I say this: You can be ruined financially without being ruined internally. You can lose everything and be okay. You will get through this. You will survive this. This isn't a financial book, so I am not going to go into too much detail here, but I am going to list some tips to help you get out of debt and stay out of debt.

1. Determine from this day forward that you will not spend more than you make. According to Ramsey Solutions, 80 percent of Americans are caught up in the chains of debt (see https://www.ramseysolutions .com/debt/americans-have-debt). That means eight out of ten of us spend more than we make. Let's stop

doing that. Every time we spend money we don't have, we pay the difference with our peace. There is a peace cost to trying to live above our means.

2. Get on a budget and stay on a budget. For years I have spoken to amazing people on the radio, and the callers always have the same tone in their voice—the tone of hopelessness. Caller after caller feels overwhelmed, not knowing where to start. Once I walk them through the process of putting together a very basic written budget, I adjust my headphones and lean in to listen to their tone change from hopeless to hopeful. Never underestimate the power of having a written plan. Without a budget, all the expenses, obligations, and due dates are just swirling around in our heads creating chaos in our souls. We would never build a house or run a company without a plan. Our personal lives should not be any different. Write out a plan and stick to it.

3. Be generous. Generosity doesn't always have to come in the form of dollars. It can come in words of encouragement, in time given, but, yes, sometimes it can take the form of money as well. The Bible tells us in Luke 6:38, "Give, and it will be given to you. A good measure, pressed down, shaken together and running over, will be poured into your lap. For with the measure you use, it will be measured to you." If we give nothing, we receive nothing. I like the way God's economy works. You don't have to start with a lot, but start a practice of generosity in your life. Not only will you be on the right side of God's generosity, but you will also be filled with joy as just a little bit of your life becomes about someone else and not your financial problems.

4

Show Up, Be a Danny

Despite my hopes for this new place, life in sunny California never felt sunny for our family. As long as I could remember, my mom had drunk alcohol excessively, but now her drinking became more and more constant, and holding down jobs became more and more difficult for her. There was a three-week period when we lived under the bridge near the corner of Edwards Street and Warner Avenue in Huntington Beach. I'm not sure what happened; I assume Mom didn't pay the rent. We were evicted from apartment 503 and went to live under the bridge. Three weeks later, we returned to the same complex, but this time we lived in apartment 217. I don't know if my dad helped us get back into an apartment or my mom secured government help. Regardless, we were back at Ocean Breeze Villas despite our recent eviction.

Only this time things were different. It started when my friend Danny and I would walk to school together. We tried our best to mind our own business and not talk to anyone but each other. But there were two large problems with this plan. Their names were José and Alejandro.

José and Alejandro were in our grade, but unbeknownst to us, they were tied to older kids in a gang. It wasn't long before they began to taunt Danny and me on the way to school. We didn't like this at all, and we tried to ignore them because José was so confident and strong, and I wasn't either of those, plus I was small for my age. They were much bigger than me. I must have made good prey because they taunted me more than Danny.

Maybe I looked more scared than I thought I was letting on and they knew it. I *was* scared, but I did everything in my power not to show it. But these bullies never let up. "Boy, one of these days I'm going to beat you up so bad you won't be able to walk home. Do you need me to call your mom and tell her you're too scared to go to school today? Should I tell her your shorts haven't fit you in two years?" Danny and I took it day after day until the day came when I just couldn't take another minute of ridicule from those jerks. José and Alejandro were about ten steps behind us, mouthing off the entire time. Without considering the outcome, I threw my bag at Danny and ran toward Alejandro, swinging as hard as I could. José must have run off because he didn't try to pull me off Alejandro and he didn't gang up on me. It was just me and Alejandro, who was about forty pounds heavier than me.

At first, I was proud of myself because I was getting in some good shots! I thought for sure I was going to teach Alejandro a lesson he'd never forget. And then the tide turned. He grabbed me around the waist and threw me backward into some bushes. He jumped on top of me and was doing a stellar job pounding my face in when the woman who owned the house whose yard we were fighting in ran out and broke things up. She threatened to call the police if we didn't promise her we would keep our hands off each other. We promised. She went inside. Alejandro looked at me with a smirk that said, "We're just getting started" and then turned and walked away laughing with José, who had reappeared.

Danny never said a word. He just stood there for a minute and then reached in his book bag and handed me his PE shirt to wipe my face. My face stung as I wiped the sweat and blood from it. My bottom lip felt puffy. Still not saying a word, Danny handed me my book bag, and we walked silently to school together. He never brought up the butt-whooping I received that day. Danny was my first real friend. Danny taught me something that day that has always stuck with me. A true friend shows up. Period.

They show up in the stadium in the front row with their face painted and a foam number one finger on their hand when it is your shining moment, but they also show up when you're facedown in the bushes. They hand you their shirt to clean yourself up with. They don't remind you of where you went wrong or how they would have done it better. They just show up. In the front row of the stadium, yes, but also in the courtroom, at the police department, at rehab.

> Danny taught me something that day that has always stuck with me. A true friend shows up. Period.

I think sometimes in our Christian circles we think it is our job to "speak truth" to people who have messed up. If there is any chance they will listen, it is our job to speak truth, to tell them where they went wrong or how they took their eyes off Jesus. After all, isn't that why Jesus probably made them our friend in the first place? He knew this moment was coming, and he wanted us there to speak truth.

I don't believe that anymore. Let me ask you, have you ever messed up badly and didn't know you messed up? Have you ever screwed up your life and thought, *I wonder where I went wrong?* or *I sure wish one of my friends would tell me exactly how badly I screwed things up*?

I have never encountered someone who has needed help figuring out how big of a mess they have made of things, but every time there has been a mess, I can assure you, I have found someone who is in desperate need of encouragement. Someone who needs to be reminded that they are not alone in the mess they've made. Someone who needs a friend to get on their knees with a few rags and help them clean up that mess. True friends cover you when you are weak and celebrate you when you are winning, but in all times, they stay. Friends show up for each other. A true friend walks in when the rest of the world walks out.

A dear friend of mine who happened to be a pastor of one of the largest churches in America for over a decade started having marriage problems. The stress of the ongoing marriage problems along with the pressure of leading a very large church began to get to him. He started drinking, and drinking too much at that. One day his board fired him as the lead pastor of the church because he had a "drinking problem." Drinking was just a symptom of much deeper problems, but that was the focus of his overseeing board and the reason they chose to let him go.

Almost immediately after this happened, my friend flew across the country and checked himself into a rehab center. I talked to him a few times during his allotted weekly phone time. During one of the calls, he told me he was finally able to have visitors the following weekend but only for a couple of hours on one specific day. Ignorantly, I said, "Oh, that's great. So, your wife will be coming to visit?"

He answered, "I doubt it. I doubt anyone will come, but I'm thankful I've made it this far. That is something to celebrate."

In that moment, my heart broke. I remembered Danny, and I felt bad that my friend didn't have one "Danny" in his life when he was facedown in the bushes. Here was this man who had loved and served a church for over a decade, who had tens of thousands attending every week to hear what he had prepared for them, and he didn't have one person who would show up and care for him in one of his darkest moments. Not one person to ask him how it was going or how he was feeling as he was adjusting to life with no church to lead while trying to salvage a broken marriage. Not. One. Person. That broke my heart. I told Holly that night that I was buying a ticket and flying across the country to see him. I took a four-hour flight and then drove another two hours to the rehab center to have a one-hour conversation with him. Then I got back in the car and made the same trip back to Nashville.

Once news spread in our circle that I had visited my friend, several friends called me and said things like, "Be careful about being publicly associated with him. It won't look good." Well, this about burned me up. Look good for who? Me? My reputation? My appearance that I am only there for people when they are at the top of their game? I don't get it. People mess up. Pastors mess up. It kills me that pastors tell the good news of God's grace every single week, but they get very little of it from others in return. I wonder if Jesus was worried about his reputation when he met with the woman at the well. Or the woman caught in adultery. Being more concerned about how I look as your friend than being your friend makes me no friend at all.

Before the trip, others told me, "I'm so glad you are going to see him so you can speak truth to him. He needs someone to speak truth to him right now." I wasn't going to speak truth. I wasn't going to not speak truth. In all honesty, I knew hardly anything about the situation, so I wasn't planning on speaking one way or the other. I was going to show him that he was not forgotten in his mess. That he had people in his life who cared about him. I was going to tell him I was proud of him for making it this far in rehab. I was going to say nothing and simply sit with him. Simply show up. I was going to do for him what Danny had done for me.

Maybe friendships haven't always been easy for you. Maybe you're like me and have often felt like you have very little to offer. You know what I've learned? I've learned that people don't really care how smart, successful, or popular you are. They just need someone who isn't afraid to show up. A friend who will show up whether they are leaning over sick in the bathroom or handcuffed in the station or weeping at the graveside. We need courtroom friends more than we need stadium friends.

I've learned that people don't really care how smart, successful, or popular you are. They just need someone who isn't afraid to show up.

Don't we all long for a friend like that? The best way to find what you long for is to be the person you long to have in your life. Don't sit back and feel the gap of a lack of friendships. Step in and fill that gap for someone else. Don't feel the gap; *fill* the gap. Be a safe place for someone to show up to. Search beyond the words they are saying to you and dig in. Ask them what they are really feeling behind their words. When they do open up with what they are struggling with, discouraged by, or afraid of, don't try to fix it. Don't start directing them immediately. Just stay in that moment and hold space for them. Very little has to be said. Simply showing up is what matters. I wonder what our friend circles would look like if we picked people up instead of walking out on them, if we were the kind of friend who walked in when everyone else walked out.

5

Feeling Stuck

José and Alejandro never beat me up again. They did introduce me to their older contacts, and if Alejandro made me nervous, this new group was terrifying. I didn't understand at first, but later I learned that José and Alejandro were tied to a gang and would connect kids our age with the older guys in the gang. I don't know if they were vetting us or initiating us or what. I just know they would tell me to be at a certain apartment after school, and I never felt like it was an invitation I could say no to. I also knew it wasn't an invitation to play mud football with my friends.

I went. Day after day. Usually to an apartment where a kid named Joby lived. Joby was my age, but he had an older sister connected to these friends of José and Alejandro. I don't know where Joby's parents were, but I never saw them once. Every time I went into Joby's apartment, it was filled with smoke. I don't know what it was. Drugs? Cigarette smoke? I always went during the after-school hours, and I was always hungry when I went over there, so maybe it was the combination of an empty stomach and whatever was in that smoke-filled apartment that made me pass out once while working on a puzzle. I woke up to a bunch of scary people standing over me, and I just wanted to cry. The place was dark. I didn't fully understand what was going on, but everyone was always whispering and being secretive. I knew we'd get in trouble if we got caught.

One afternoon a police officer came and arrested at least twelve people at the apartment. Joby, José, Alejandro, and I didn't get arrested. A police officer took us to a quiet space outside and told us we needed to stay away from these older people because they were doing bad things. I wanted to tell him we didn't have a choice! I said nothing. I was scared. But I did try to decline the invitation a couple of times, and that ended with a beating. I learned very quickly that the choice was to show up where they said or get beat up. So, I went. Day after day I went and hung out in disgusting, dark apartments. I was stuck and had no idea how to get out of this situation.

I got my location instructions every day from José on the way home from school. He would tell me exactly where to be and how much time I had to get there. There were usually several people shooting, snorting, and smoking when I arrived. They seemed to have code names, or maybe they were names for drugs I just didn't know at that time. Most of the time the older kids would let me say "No thanks" to the drugs and just taunt me for a minute and then move on, but as I spent more and more afternoons with them, they began to get aggressive about me trying drugs. One day they were relentless. I was scared. Scared to do drugs and scared to get beat up if I didn't. So I did what any kid would do: I faked smoking a joint. I'm sure it was the poorest attempt at faking it in the history of ever.

The guys were beyond aggravated. They grabbed me by the arms and dragged me to the parking garage located below the apartments. One guy picked me up and slammed me on the back of an old car and tried to force me to inhale. "You better smoke this joint right now, boy, or you will be so sorry." I was angry by this point. I shook my head no and clenched my lips closed. Three other gang members were watching this go down, and when they saw me disrespect their leader, they got in my face and said, "No one disrespects us, you idiot." They grabbed me off the car and threw me behind it. I started kicking and screaming with everything in me. One guy held my legs, while another put one hand on my chest and one on my head in a way that pinned the back of my head between the ground and the right rear tire. Another guy got in the car and aggressively revved the engine. It was so loud. They were laughing hysterically, and I was hysterically crying. I thought I was going to die.

While my head was pinned behind the tire, the driver shifted the car and let it rock just a little while revving the engine. As the car rocked backward on my head, it tore hair from my scalp. I thought it was all over. I was screaming in terror, "Please stop! Please! Please stop!" When the fun was over for them, they picked me up and threw me on the back of the car. They were still laughing. I had tears streaming down my face. I smoked my first joint right then and there. From then on, I smoked a joint every time they told me to. I was stuck.

I didn't tell my mom what happened that day until months later when the final straw happened. There was a bridge near the apartment complex, and a mattress was tucked under it. At the bottom of the hill under the bridge was a ravine. I'm not exactly sure what was going on there except to say that we were in one of the poorest neighborhoods in town, and there was most definitely human feces in the water below the bridge. You could smell it from the apartment complex. One afternoon a couple of the older guys and a girl took me under the bridge to that mattress and started fondling me. I tried to squirm away because I didn't like it, I was scared, and I wasn't sure what they were going to do next. I almost got away, but the two older boys caught me as I tried to run home. They dragged me down to that sewer water, forced my head under the water, and held it there. I came out gasping for air and smelling like human feces. I vomited. I cried. They laughed. I ran home screaming. Mom was not there and wouldn't be home for hours. I was so afraid they would come back and get me that I locked the door and hid in the bathroom until my mom got home. I was too scared even to take a shower because I was afraid they would come in the apartment while I was in the shower. I hated this place, but I knew we had nowhere else to go. We were stuck.

I didn't know what to do with all of this as a young boy. I knew Mom couldn't take us somewhere else, but I honestly thought I was going to get killed if we stayed. I had never been so afraid, not even the night my mom's boyfriend had held Joel and that knife. When my mom got home that night, I cried and cried. Between sobs, I somehow stammered out everything that had been happening to me after school. I told her how afraid I was that they would kill me. Mom cried. Joel played on the floor and ate Cheerios, oblivious to what was going on. Mom told me to take a good, long shower while she put Joel to bed. When I was done with my shower, Mom was sitting on the couch staring blankly at the wall above the TV that sat on the floor of our living room. She looked up at me and said, "I'm getting us out of here. I am going to find a way. You are not staying another night in this apartment."

And I never did.

My mom sent me immediately to my dad's house for a few nights while she figured things out. I just hung out by myself at Dad's house while he went to work. He had the nicest house I had ever been in, so I didn't mind at all. I just locked myself inside, climbed in my dad's maroon recliner, and watched TV all day. I watched *Ferris Bueller's Day Off* and *Short Circuit* on TBS numerous times that week. Within a few days, Mom came by and told me that she had called her sister in Florida. My aunt and her husband were separated, but my aunt said my uncle would fly to California and drive my mom and Joel across the country to Venice, Florida, where they would stay at his house until my mom could get her feet back under her. I stayed with my dad for about a week and then flew by myself to Florida to meet up with them. That was the summer before eighth grade. I was thirteen years old, and I remember sitting alone on the plane prior to takeoff scared to death the gang members would burst through the door and take me. Once the plane took off, I started to relax, but then I realized I had never been on a plane in my life, and I was slightly scared to fly in that thing. It didn't take me long to calm my nerves about flying, and soon I relaxed at the thought that I never had to see any of those awful people again. For the first time in a long time, I didn't feel stuck.

I sat there dreaming of what was next. I'd never been to Florida. I'd never even met my uncle until a few days earlier. He seemed nice. He had a big smile. I thought he must be rich because he had flown all the way to California from Florida. I wondered if he would be nice to us. Even if he wasn't, it would still be better than what we were leaving, and I was really good at staying out of the way of adults who weren't nice. I decided right then and there that no matter what, Florida was going to be better than California.

One thing that was nagging at the back of my mind as I waited for the flight attendant to bring me my ginger ale was something I had heard my dad say a few days earlier. I had overheard him refer to my mom as a drunk when he was on the phone, and although I didn't have the vocabulary for it, I knew deep down she was becoming more and more addicted to alcohol, and more depressed. I knew that although we were moving across the country, her eyes were still empty. Maybe she, too, felt stuck. Not in a location like I had but to a bottle. Stuck with no way out. I felt sad for my mom because I knew she was not happy, but she was my hero. She had saved me from the gang. She had protected me. She was in the process of changing her whole world to make me a better one. But her eyes made me think that her world wasn't getting any better.

I've seen the same look—the look of deep hopelessness, the look of feeling completely and utterly stuck—in so many since seeing it daily in my mom's eyes as a child.

When Holly and I were just getting into ministry, we lived near her family in their hometown of Charlotte, North Carolina. One miserably cold, sleeting January day, a pastor from sunny south Florida called me and said that God kept laying my name on his heart and asked if I would be interested in considering a pastoral position on his team. He went on to explain that he wanted to treat Holly and me to a weekend in south Florida to visit his church and discuss an opportunity he had available for me there. Honestly, I wasn't interested in a pastoral position on his team, but I was interested in a weekend in sunny south Florida. I mean, it was cloudy and twenty-one degrees in Charlotte when he called, and it was seventy-four degrees and sunny in Florida that day. We had two toddlers at the time and a baby on the way. To be honest, you could have asked me to come pursue an opportunity to clean porta potties at the local fairgrounds and I would have gone just to get a weekend in the sun away from toddlers with just Holly and me. Holly and I were on a plane headed his way the following weekend. Although we had little interest in moving, we loved our local church and were very interested in seeing what God was up to at this one.

We spent all weekend with the pastor and his wife. After each service, meeting, or meal with the staff, Holly and I would quickly debrief in the elevator at the hotel as we headed to our room. She'd ask me the same question every time. "On a scale of 1 to 10, where are you at with this possibility?" I'd say zero every time, and she would sigh a deep sigh of relief and say, "Oh, good. Me too."

That was until the final service on the final day. The pastor took us to his most diverse campus. The campus had been struggling for a while and was on the brink of shutting its doors. The chairs were divided into three sections in the auditorium, and we sat in the far-right section in the second row. After the first two songs, the worship leader asked us to take a moment to say hello to someone in the room. There weren't many of us, so it was a bit awkward. I walked across the aisle to the middle section of chairs, where there seemed to be a few more people than in our section. I spotted a woman standing about two rows behind us with several children, maybe four or five, at her side. I went to her, and when she turned to me, I saw the look. The look of hopelessness that I had seen in my mom. The look that comes when opportunities are limited. The look I felt inside when I had been stuck. Her eyes told me she was stuck. Stuck with a handful of little ones depending on her. Stuck with exhaustion and stress tempting her to find a way to numb herself. I knew that look too well.

In an instant, my heart broke for her. For her kids. For the lack of hope that was sucking the life out of her and making her barely able to hold her head up. She didn't need me, but she needed Jesus, and I knew right then and there that I could bring Jesus to her. I hugged her and told her to hold on. She started sobbing in my arms. I, too, started crying. She held on to my shoulders and wouldn't let go. When the moment was over, I walked back to my seat next to Holly. She didn't say a word, but about ten minutes later when we finally sat down and I stopped shedding tears for this woman, she wrote on the church program, "So we are moving here, aren't we?" Six weeks later, we lived in sunny south Florida, and I was the pastor of that campus. It was one of the best decisions we ever made.

Jesus became so real and alive to us at that campus. I never saw that woman with all the children again, but I pray she stepped through our doors and I just happened to miss her the next time she came. She helped me make a decision that changed my life and my family's life, and that little ole church that had an empty parking lot for decades on end began to bust at the seams. Broken people finding wholeness and healing. Stressed people finding peace. People who felt like nothing in life was making sense or had any meaning finding purpose in building a community they and others could belong to. People needing another chance at life and finding a God just waiting to show them his love and give them that chance. God used this young man who didn't know much at all, but what he did know was how to recognize the pain of feeling stuck. The pain of hopelessness. I knew the answer to that pain wasn't found in a bottle or a pill but in Jesus. The experience in that church taught me that I want to give my life to seeing pain and relieving pain by bringing people to Jesus.

> I knew the answer to that pain wasn't found in a bottle or a pill but in Jesus.

Does hopelessness have a hold on you? Do you feel stuck? Like opportunities just don't come around for people like you? Maybe it's something else. Maybe you feel stuck because a bill is overdue and you have no way to pay it. Because false rumors have been spread about you and everyone is believing the worst. Because a spouse has told you the relationship is over. Stuck. With no possible way to fix the situation you are in. There's no magic pill to take, no class to attend, no habit to stop doing.

There is a story in the book of Exodus that I didn't learn about until much later in my life, but it really helps me understand what might be happening in God's world while I am feeling stuck in my world. Hopefully, it'll help you as well. Hang with me as I give you a little synopsis of the historical landscape at the time of this story.

The nation of Israel had served as slaves in the country of Egypt for four hundred years. Then God worked on Israel's behalf, and Egypt let the entire nation of Israel leave the country to find their own personal freedom and national independence. The Israelites marched out of Egypt, and the Bible tells us they were following God to a special land—a land that God himself had chosen just for them. Oftentimes when people speak of this special land for Israel, they refer to it as the promised land . . . and I like that because Israel serves as a model for us.

Their life as a nation actually mirrors a lot of the ups and downs we all go through as we make our faith journeys. So, when you hear "promised land" in your head, you could say "purpose." If you grew up Baptist, you could say "calling," or if you grew up charismatic, you could say "destiny." Promised land, purpose, calling, destiny—they essentially mean the same thing: coming to a place in your life that you discovered and where you are living out what God made you for.

As God led Israel on the path to discovering this promised land, the coolest thing happened for them: "The LORD went ahead of them. He guided them during the day with a pillar of cloud, and he provided light at night with a pillar of fire. . . . And the LORD did not remove the pillar of cloud or pillar of fire from its place in front of the people" (Exod. 13:21–22 NLT).

Now that is like the real-life version of asking God to write his direction in the clouds and he does it! This cloud literally went ahead of them and showed them each and every step to take. Don't you just wish we had a cloud like that? Do I take this job or that one? Well, which company is the cloud hovering over? Do we have another child, or is two enough? Well, the cloud is over the laundry baskets full of dirty laundry, so that's a definite no. That cloud would be awesome! Israel had such a cloud, and as long as they followed it, they could be assured they were on the right path to their destiny.

Look where this cloud led Israel next: "Then the LORD gave these instructions to Moses: 'Order the Israelites to turn back and camp by Pi-hahiroth between Migdol and the sea. Camp there along the shore, across from Baal-zephon'" (Exod. 14:1–2 NLT). The two words in there that are difficult to pronounce—Pi-hahiroth and Baal-zephon—are mountains, so essentially, God led Israel into a valley with a mountain range on their right, a mountain range on their left, and the Red Sea in front of them.

All the while, the Egyptians were watching Israel closely because they were having second thoughts about letting them go free. When they realized Israel was cornered, they decided to recapture their free laborers. Israel looked back, and they could see the Egyptian army closing in on them. Israel was in serious trouble. It was like driving up to a raised drawbridge with Lake Superior on either side of you and a car full of gang members chasing you.

If you continue reading the story, you see that God stepped in and did a miraculous thing—he rescued Israel. What we assume was a moment of being completely and utterly stuck was exactly that—just a moment. The Israelites' situation looked hopeless. Moses, their leader, calmed them all down, prayed, held out his staff, and bam! The sea parted, and the Israelites walked through. But as the Egyptians followed, the water came crashing down and drowned them. An hour tops and—whew!—the threat was over.

But what happens in our lives today when a moment is not a moment but a month or a year? Or two or three? How do we live there? It's like someone hits pause on the worst scene of our lives. And just like that we are stuck. Are you stuck in one of the most difficult times of your life?

Your husband is not coming home, but you desperately don't want a divorce. Stuck.

The cancer did not go away with the chemo, and there is nothing more they can do. Stuck.

They will never forgive you, and you are racked with guilt and regret. Stuck.

They aren't sure how long your father has. Stuck.

The money is gone, the foreclosure has started, and the bankruptcy is underway, but the court date is nine months away. Stuck.

We could find comfort in moments like these if we could just get some kind of sign that God is in control *and* that he is with us. We need to know that he has not left us to survive this alone. We want to look up and see that pillar of cloud, right? We need a sign.

Have you ever prayed that? "God, I need a sign from you." Have you ever begged for his manifest presence, some kind of physical evidence or a felt experience that makes it crystal clear that God is present and active? The cloud was that for Israel.

What's your cloud? It could be a friend who calls out of the blue and says, "I just had this really strong sense to give you a call to remind you that you are going to make it." Maybe you've had a cloud moment while listening to worship music. You had this sense of confidence and courage that you didn't have before. Maybe a stranger pays for your coffee, and you just know that God is telling you your finances are in his control.

The manifested presence of God often comes through a timely word, an act of kindness, something you experience inside you that assures you God is with you. As I was writing that very sentence on a hotel balcony on Sanibel Island overlooking the water, God sent a cloud via a text message to my phone. Out of the corner of my left eye, I saw my phone light up with a new message from a random friend from nine years ago who wrote, "How are you guys? I wanted to ask . . . I know you two are setting up a church, and it is all probably still in the infancy. But I truly believe in your ministry. I usually donate to church through PushPay. Are you guys set up through that by chance? I was hoping I could tithe there for you as well. Thank you."

I'm literally typing through blurry eyes right now as I silently weep. What the friend doesn't know (but God does) is that I just signed a lease on a big church building yesterday that was a huge faith step, and I am trusting God that he will continue to bless Holly's and my efforts as we seek to serve our hometown through the vehicle of a local church. The building size is significant, and so is the monthly lease amount, but we believe in this so much that we're willing to step up in the event the church can't afford it. Time and time again over the last three weeks of our church's infancy, God has sent cloud after cloud to let us know that he is with us and that we're on the right path.

Surely, as Israel's enemy was closing in on them, they simply looked up and saw their assurance. They saw their cloud, right? But look what happens: "Then the angel of God, who had been leading the people of Israel, moved to the rear of the camp. The pillar of cloud also moved from the front and stood behind them" (Exod. 14:19 NLT). The cloud left and went behind them. What they always looked to for assurance of God's presence was now gone. I mean . . . just when you think things can't get worse, your cloud disappears!

The friends quit calling. The worship music is just words going in one ear and out the other. You are so panicked that you aren't hearing anything from God. No cloud. You are stuck with no assurance that God is with you.

It is so easy in moments like this to think the worst. *Certainly, I misunderstood God's directions, and now I'm doomed.* Doomed for divorce. Doomed for the business to fail. Or maybe you begin to think that God is punishing you for screwing things up years ago. And in a moment of panic, instead of keeping your focus on God's faithfulness to you, you put the focus on your unfaithfulness to him. When you need reassurance the *most* that you and God are in this together, you suddenly feel at odds with God. You can't see his presence. You have been unfaithful to him, so therefore he must be against you.

But what we so easily forget is that God led Israel right to this moment. He led them there, and even though his presence shifted, he did *not* leave them. God was still there; it was just different.

It is the same with your situation. God has not left you alone in your stuck moment. He's still there! He is not at odds with you! But why would he not allow you in a moment of great fear to see him in the ways you always have?

> God has not left you alone in your stuck moment. He's still there!

I think we find the answer in Exodus 14:19–20: "The pillar of cloud also moved from in front and stood behind them, coming between the armies of Egypt and Israel. Throughout the night the cloud brought darkness to the one side and light to the other side; so neither went near the other all night long." In this moment, God went from guiding Israel to protecting them. Could he do both at the same time? Sure! But maybe this moment was more about teaching his people than proving his abilities. They had already come to know God as their guide. Maybe in this moment he wanted them to know him as their protector. Sometimes we want God's guidance, and he wants us to know his protection!

Holly and I now live on a small hobby farm in Tennessee. I love spending time working on the farm. Most days I'm up long before Holly and the kids, and I head outside to work and watch the sunrise. Holly says that sometimes I am out there for eight hours before I come in, but I'm not sure I believe that. She asks me all the time, "So what exactly do you do out there?" And most days I don't know how to answer her because, honestly, it's just a lot of piddling around. Repairing this and cleaning that. She reminds me often that we aren't *real* farmers, since we have very few animals (and they are all pets, not dinner) and no crops. Real farmer or not, I love my time outside. And since I often leave my phone inside when I am out working, Holly told me this recently: "I sometimes wonder if you are out there or if maybe you have left and gone somewhere. But you know how I know you are here? Your truck. I'm constantly peeking around the farm for your truck." I drive an old red truck, and I haul that thing all over the farm. Down to the pond, out to the back field, or even to the barn if I need to get some hay to our horses. You see, as long as Holly looks out the window in her home office and sees that red truck, she might not know where on the farm I am, but she knows I am there somewhere. I haven't left.

As much as I wish it were so, I am not just a hobby farmer. I'm also a pastor, ministry coach, and speaker. Of course, when I am traveling for a speaking engagement, Holly will look out her window and not see my truck. Now, what if in that moment, when I am actually doing the job that provides for our family, Holly assumes that because she doesn't see my truck, I have left her for good? What if she assumes that I have abandoned our family? That I have left her to raise three kids alone. That I am against her all of a sudden. That I am out to take every penny I can from her.

If Holly did that, you would tell me that she is crazy, and I would agree! When she doesn't see my truck, it isn't that I have left her. It's that in that moment this wannabe hobby farmer is out providing for the wife and kids I love so much. I'm securing our future. I'm doing my best to make sure our kids have clothes on their bodies and braces on their teeth. Just because she can't see my truck doesn't mean I left her or gave up on her. And that's because I am not only a hobby farmer but also the provider for our family.

The same is true about our God. When his presence in your life shifts, maybe it's because there's another side of him he wants you to get to know. Because the Bible says this:

The LORD your God, He is the One who goes with you. He will not leave you nor forsake you. (Deut. 31:6 NKJV)

When you go through deep waters, I will be with you. (Isa. 43:2 NLT)

And be sure of this: I am with you always, even to the end of the age. (Matt. 28:20 NLT)

You may be in a situation today where there is a sea in front of you, a mountain on either side, and the enemy closing in behind you. It may seem like every trace of God has vanished, and you find yourself wondering if you have been forsaken. You can stand strong because you know that God's presence is not dependent on your ability to see it. It's dependent on his inability to break his promises.

When we stand confident when the rest of the world has caved in to fear or thrown in the towel, when we stand in the gap when everyone has told us we should walk away, when we stand firm, we can see hopeless circumstances changed, callous hearts softened, and opportunities provided that never would have come if we hadn't trusted and waited. Hold on. God is with you. You are never stuck when you have God.

6

Shame Off You

For the first few years after my mom, Joel, and I moved to Florida, life was a fairy tale compared to life in California. We had a stable place to live with my uncle. He was super tidy, and I knew that we were imposing on him, so I was careful to be on my best behavior at all times: I carried a drink with two hands. I was careful not to drag my fingers along the wall when walking down the hallway. I took my shoes off before coming inside. I think my mom must have felt the same way and was also on her best behavior because her drinking slowed way down while we were there. Or maybe it slowed because she didn't feel overwhelmed or scared like she did when we were on our own. Regardless of why, she wasn't drinking as much, and the first two years in Florida felt peaceful and safe. It was the first time I can remember feeling that way. At night, I went to bed dreaming about the fish I would catch with my uncle the next day or the baseball game I was going to hit a home run in that upcoming weekend.

Restored

I'd always been a shy kid, but the events in California shut me down even more socially. I didn't talk to anyone, really. I simply went to school, did what I was told, and played any and every sport I could get my mom to agree to. My uncle also taught math at my school, so he saw me in my social setting; he observed how shut off I was and how I simply sat back in the corner and watched everyone else engaging with each other. He stepped in and helped me. He taught me how to navigate conflict without getting so angry, how to approach a teacher and ask a question if I didn't understand, how to discover things I had in common with other kids and then use those things to start a conversation. He knew I needed help, and because I really wanted to please him, I tried what he taught me. He taught me a lot about manhood, like how to tie my first tie, how to drive a stick shift, how to dock a boat, how to shoot a gun, and how to bait and clean a fish. These little lessons helped me gain confidence, and I began to discover that I might, just might, be able to make it in the big world one day.

With no violence in our lives, I was able to focus on things normal young teens focused on. I discovered that I really liked baseball and that I was pretty good at it. I wasn't great, but I was good enough to make a couple all-star teams. My mom said she couldn't pay for baseball and wouldn't be able to drive me to practices or games since she worked multiple jobs, so I got my first job when I was fourteen so I could earn money and pay my way to play. I worked pulling weeds for a lady named Ms. Anne. She paid me three dollars and fifty cents an hour. I paid for my baseball fees and necessary equipment with the money, and any extra I gave to my mom.

After about two years in Florida, Mom and my uncle started to argue quite a bit. I always thought it was due to

72

the fact that my uncle was so disciplined and tidy, and my mom would push his limits. She would do something she *knew* he wouldn't like, like leave dirty dishes in the sink overnight. Then he would of course say something about it, and she would start up. She would get inches from his face and say, "You just think you're so much better than me, don't you? That you got your life perfectly together and I can't even afford a place of my own." I hated when she did this. It scared me because my uncle was letting us live with him, and I really didn't want to go back to the shelters or under a bridge. But she was really good at making him mad. I would try to distract my mom so she would stop taunting him into starting an argument. I'd ask her if she could come to a game soon or if she wanted to go for a walk together. Anything I could think of to get her to focus on anything besides my uncle and the way she felt unworthy around him. I don't know if it was the shame of how her life was turning out or if the frequent arguing was too much, but Mom just started to cave. I'm not exactly sure why, but Mom began to self-sabotage and ruin the safest living situation we had ever had.

By the end of our third year in Florida, we had left my uncle's house and moved into a cheap apartment on our own. Almost immediately, Mom started drinking heavily again. Consequently, keeping a job became more and more difficult. With every job loss, she seemed to sink deeper and deeper into the dark hole of addiction. We didn't have much when we lived with my uncle, but now we had nothing except food for us . . . and alcohol and cigarettes for Mom. Mom had qualified us for food stamps, so at least we had food in our cupboards, unlike in California, where the only things emptier than the kitchen cabinets were our stomachs.

By this point, I had found an outlet for my anger, fear, and frustrations by playing high school baseball. I started to realize that, postpuberty, my "mysterious ball player" reputation was starting to work in my favor. I don't know why, maybe I was afraid of anyone getting too close to me or maybe I just liked the attention of several girls and not just one (I know, that made me a player), but I dated a lot of girls. But rarely did they come to my house, and never ever did I open up and tell them about my real life off the baseball field. That was off-limits. Everyone knew my life off the field wasn't pretty, but *no one* knew what I had come from and how dark my mom's battles could get.

It was about this same time in high school that I started to resent my mom. I wanted so badly for things to go right in my world, and I kept thinking she was the one making them go wrong. I was embarrassed to be on "free lunches." Since I got free lunches, she wouldn't let me pack a lunch and waste the food at home. I remember being too embarrassed to swipe my card in front of the girls I wanted desperately to impress, so I would just skip lunch and say I wasn't hungry. I did that for about three days and then almost passed out in baseball practice, so I decided I'd just have to be embarrassed and get some food. But the embarrassment made me upset with my mom, and so did the fact that I had given her all the extra money I had earned from jobs since I was fourteen. I hated that I always smelled like smoke because my mom had a cigarette burning in every room in our house at all times. I was disgusted to smell like that, and I resented her for it. I resented the fact that my brother, Joel, and I were on a first-name basis with every cop in town. I'd go to a grocery store or gas station, and a police officer would say, "Hi, Chris. How ya doing?" What they really meant was, "How's your mom? Are you guys in a bad situation? Need our help?"

It wasn't long after moving out of my uncle's house that Mom started dating another guy, and soon we moved into a cheap duplex with him. I was in the eleventh grade at this point. Mom and I were fighting a lot. I remember getting so mad at her one night because all my feelings of being embarrassed came to the surface. I was embarrassed by the way I had to smell at school, by having to swipe my free lunch card, and by being the kid all the teachers knew had a "tough life." I hated it all, and the anger built up so much that I punched a large ashtray on the coffee table, leaving my hand sliced up and bleeding. I got several stitches that night. That was the night I learned that anger may prove your point, but it will likely cost you something in return.

After this, I learned to "run" when I got overwhelmed with anger toward my mom. I would walk right out of the house without saying a word and would head to my friend Justin's house. Once, I woke up ticked in the middle of the night because I heard my mom stumbling in drunk yet again. I got up, told her what I thought of her, and then left and knocked on Justin's door. His grandma answered, and I explained that I needed a place to crash because my mom and I were fighting. She said she couldn't let me stay there because a mom and her son must stick together. She told me I needed to go home and figure it out with my mom, and then she simply shut the door in my face. It was two o'clock in the morning, and I was *not* going back home. It was Florida, and salamanders and armadillos are a very real thing. And so are bad people in gangs who do drugs and shove your head under car tires. I would never have admitted it, but I was scared. I had done the bridge thing plenty of times, but

I had always had my mom with me. I had never been alone outside all night before.

After thinking through my options, I figured I had only three hours until it would be light, so I'd just find a place nearby where no person or animal could see me and I'd crash there. I tried to open Justin's grandma's van and sneak in there, but it was locked. The grass was soaking wet with dew, so that wasn't an option. I didn't want to lie on the front porch and have someone drive by and see me. I couldn't think of what to do, so in my brilliance, I climbed under the van to hide myself from passersby, armadillos, and drug lords and slept fitfully on my back for a few hours. It was tight quarters, but I made it. As I lay under that car, I couldn't help but remind myself of the promise I had made in that California apartment on my eleventh birthday: I will never be like my mom when I get older. I will be rich. I will be like my rich dad, and I'll never have to do things like this again.

As I was navigating the turbulent waters of life with someone who struggles with addiction, I was learning that the baseball field was a much better place to release my anger than a coffee table. I loved that I could throw a baseball as hard as I wanted and would never get anything but compliments for it. At this point, I still had the deal with my mom that I could play ball as long as I handled my ride situations and paid for it, except now there was a new caveat: I had to take my brother, Joel, with me anywhere I went after school was over. She couldn't pay childcare, and he wasn't old enough to stay home while she waited tables. I didn't know what I was going to do with him because I played on the school baseball team and we traveled as a team on a bus to games. What was I going to do with a seven-year-old brother?!

I went to my coach and explained the situation: I can play, but my brother is a constant tagalong. All practices. All games. He has to come with me. At the time, I thought my coach miraculously said yes because I was just that good, but now I know that word about my troubled home life had traveled around our small town pretty quickly, and Coach felt bad for me. Or maybe he knew baseball was my only outlet. The only place in my world where I didn't feel less than the people around me. The only time I felt like an equal, like a contributor to something other than my mom's funds for alcohol and cigarettes. Regardless of what prompted him, Coach allowed Joel to ride the bus to games with me.

While I played baseball all four years of high school, I didn't really make a big splash until my senior year. I had been begging Coach for a couple of years to let me pitch in a game, but I never once got an outing. I was so frustrated because I knew if I was going to go anywhere with baseball, pitching was my best shot, and he wouldn't give me a chance to prove myself. Finally, just a couple of games into my senior year, Coach told me I was going to be the starting pitcher. I was thrilled. I had been dreaming of this moment! I stood on the mound, and in my high school baseball pitching debut, I threw a no-hitter. I played it off like I had done it a million times before, but inside I was screaming with excitement! I did it! Being the hero for my team that night was the best feeling I'd ever felt. I got a second outing shortly after that one, and sure enough, I threw another no-hitter. Back-to-back no-hitters. I was on the front page of every newspaper in our small town.

We were only a few games into the season, and I was already being mentioned as a strong contender for "Florida Player of the Year." Scouts were showing up at all my games.

I was bubbling with pride on the inside, but on the outside I showed very little emotion. I was the quiet, mysterious kid—who also just happened to be the hero of the baseball team. I liked being the hero. I decided that I preferred being noticed for what good I accomplished rather than pitied for the troubled home in which I lived. I liked this new role I had been given, and now I just had to keep living up to it.

My mom had never been to one of my high school games, but once she saw her son plastered all over the newspapers and being the talk of our small town, she decided she was going to watch me play. I was coming off the rush of two no-hitters, and I was thrilled to be on the field again. I wasn't pitching because they were giving my arm a rest, but I didn't care. I was catching, and I had one goal: I was going to prove to everyone there that night that I was the MVP of the Lemon Bay baseball team. The stands were filled. The game got off to a good start. In the second inning, I noticed my mom pull up. I was excited. I was going to hit a homer for her to see. But it didn't take but one glance at my mom for me to realize she wasn't walking but rather stumbling her way up the walkway to the bleachers.

My stomach dropped as I suddenly knew this would not be good. And my stomach was right. It took only a few minutes of my mom being there for my whole world to come crashing down on me. She was drunk and swaying as she stood by the bleachers. Within moments, she started hollering, "Come on, number sixteen! Let's go, number sixteen! Look at that catcher . . . doesn't he have a cute butt?" She was slurring her words. She was loud, boisterous, and inappropriate. While everyone else grew quiet in the awkwardness, she got louder. Until it was completely silent except for Mom. And she just didn't stop. "Come on, sixteen! You are looking good! I know everyone here knows how good you look in your uniform!" she obnoxiously bellowed. I wanted to crawl in a hole and die.

After what felt like forever, some administrators approached my mom and escorted her off the property. They stayed with her in the parking lot because she was obviously drunk, and they weren't going to let her drive home. I don't know if they called the police or a taxi . . . all I know is that even from the parking lot she kept hollering toward the field: "That's my boy! You can't remove me from watching my boy!" Shame. Embarrassment. All the rumors everyone had heard about my life felt confirmed in that moment. I was the kid from the drunk home. The one you will never want your kids to hang around with. The one you'll never let your daughter date. I had finally accomplished enough for my mom to actually show up to a game, and that turned out to be more than humiliating for me.

Shame. It's a feeling I'm familiar with, but I hate it. I hate the way it makes you wish you could just make yourself invisible. I hate the way it puts a stamp on you that you feel is forever attached to your self-worth. I hate the way it makes you feel so alone in those moments. No one seems to be carrying the weight with you. You feel isolated. Humiliated. Less than.

My mom lived with so much shame, and I did too. The smell of my clothes, the swiping of my free lunch card, paying at the grocery store with food stamps, Mom showing up to the game drunk. So much shame. You know how I identify a shameful moment? When you think about it, you say, "I'd never write that in a book" or "I'd never tell my friends about that moment." Those things you just want to bury and never ever want to bring up again typically have great shame attached to them.

How about you? Do you struggle with shame? Do you have parts of you that you keep hidden but when you think of them they bring back those same feelings: isolation, humiliation, or less than? Has shame kept you from fully living life? Has it kept you hidden? Sometimes our shame is caused by what we've done and other times by what has been done to us. But I am convinced that while we think we don't want anyone to know about our shame, in truth, we are all desperately searching for people who can handle the most shameful parts of us and still love us. That is what would make us feel loved, accepted, and not alone. We feel like someone doesn't truly know us until they know the parts we hide from everyone else.

I am convinced that while we think we don't want anyone to know about our shame, in truth, we are all desperately searching for people who can handle the most shameful parts of us and still love us.

I want to show you something I learned several years ago. I want to holler with excitement when I think about what Jesus does with our shame. John 9:1–9 says:

As he went along, he saw a man blind from birth. His disciples asked him, "Rabbi, who sinned, this man or his parents, that he was born blind?"

"Neither this man nor his parents sinned," said Jesus, "but this happened so that the works of God might be displayed in him. As long as it is day, we must do the works of him who sent me. Night is coming, when no one can work. While I am in the world, I am the light of the world."

After saying this, he spit on the ground, made some mud with the saliva, and put it on the man's eyes. "Go," he told him, "wash in the Pool of Siloam" (this word means "Sent"). So the man went and washed, and came home seeing.

His neighbors and those who had formerly seen him begging asked, "Isn't this the same man who used to sit and beg?" Some claimed that he was.

Others said, "No, he only looks like him."

But he himself insisted, "I am the man."

So, quick recap: Jesus is walking. (I love that Jesus did multiple things at one time. He was heading somewhere, he was usually teaching as he went, and he often embraced the opportunity to heal along the way. He was the ultimate maximizer.) As he is walking with his best friends, they see a blind man, and Jesus decides to heal this man in a very unconventional way. Look at verse 6 again: "After saying this, he spit on the ground, made some mud with the saliva, and put it on the man's eyes." Now, why do you suppose Jesus did that? I'm asking a question; I don't know the answer. It's interesting because Jesus healed other blind men just by speaking. He called Lazarus back from the dead by speaking. One word from Jesus and everything changes. So why the spit? Good thing this gentleman couldn't see what Jesus was doing or he probably would have objected. "I'm good, Jesus. I thought maybe you were going to do like you did with everyone else and simply tell me to be healed or let me touch your clothes. I didn't realize I was going to get mudballs in my face. I'm good. Thanks anyway."

It's difficult to look at how Jesus performed this miracle and not object. It seems harmful to rub mud made with spit in a man's eyes. Unsanitary, to say the least . . .

But I want to propose something to you. I thought this was offensive at first myself—and then my wife explained something to me from her short-lived nursing career. She explained that DNA is the set of traits, qualities, or features that characterize a person. It's what makes your eyes blue, your hair dark, your skin olive, your second toe longer than your first toe. Essentially, DNA is what makes you . . . you.

Now, if someone wanted to prove that your kids are in fact your biological kids, you know what they would do? They would take your child's DNA and test it because their DNA would contain your essence. *And* this is where it gets good: Did you know the most common way to do DNA testing is with saliva?

Just go with me for a moment here. Could it be that in this moment of using his *saliva* to heal this man, Jesus was illustrating, not only to this man but also to all of us who would later have the scientific knowledge to understand, exactly what he came to do for all of us on this earth? You see, being blind was shameful for this man. It's why the disciples ignorantly asked in verse 2, "Rabbi, who sinned, this man or his parents, that he was born blind?" Being blind had caused this man to be a beggar. It probably made him do things neither he nor his parents ever thought he would have to do just to survive. His shame was created by his circumstances, but I can tell you this man felt isolated, humiliated, and less than.

But Jesus's answer to the disciples' question of who had sinned, this man or his parents, and caused his shame is found in verse 3: "'Neither this man nor his parents sinned,' said Jesus, 'but this happened so that the works of God might be displayed in him.'" Could it simply be that when Jesus wiped the mud made of dirt and spit on his eyes, he was saying, "I cover you. I cover your shame. The very essence of who I am covers the most shameful parts of you."

Jesus wants to take our shame and replace it with himself, with his essence. His essence covers. His essence heals. But often we allow the enemy to convince us that although our sins are forgiven, our shame is still our problem to carry. This holds us back from so much in life. Sin may trip us up for a season, but it is often the shame that follows that holds us down for a lifetime.

Maybe you are allowing your shame to paralyze you. To strip you of your dreams. Do you trust God enough to secure your eternity but not enough to free you of your shame? Are you still punishing yourself instead of stepping toward what God might want to do through you in this life? You do not have to be defined by that shameful thing that happened to you or that shameful thing you did.

> Sin may trip us up for a season, but it is often the shame that follows that holds us down for a lifetime.

As a teenager trying to hide from the world the reality of who I really was, I didn't have any idea that I could do something with my shame other than hide it. Hide my free lunch card. Hide my smelly clothes. Hide my drunk mom. But I later learned that when Jesus died on the cross two thousand years ago, he didn't only die for my sins. He died for my shame as well, and he did the same for you. Your shame can be covered by Jesus. Your shame can be healed by Jesus. He wants to take your past shame and make it into something beautiful today.

7

Rejection to Acceptance

Life at home didn't take long to go from bad to worse. Mom and the boyfriend we were living with broke up, and we were out of the house. But not to worry, because Mom met a guy named Geoff at the bar where she waited tables, and just three weeks after they met, we moved in with him. Geoff had one of the nicest houses I can remember us living in. It had a tile floor instead of linoleum, it had a one-car garage, and Joel and I each had our own room. I loved the house, but I didn't like Geoff. Not one bit. He was not a good guy. As angry and frustrated as I got with my mom, I always thought she was a good person who just had dark struggles. The same was true about my dad: I thought he was a good person who just made some bad choices. But I never felt that way about Geoff. From the very beginning, I thought Geoff was a bad person who did bad things, and it made me angry that my mom would choose for us to live with this man.

I'll never forget one day shortly after we moved in. I was checking the mail, and a box of checks had arrived. I opened them up to see what design my mom had chosen, and there in the top left corner of the checks I saw both of their names as an official couple. Seriously, she'd known this guy for a month! All I could think was, *Here we go again.*

Geoff and Mom were terrible for each other. Her addiction went from bad to worse during this time. The cycle of leaving to find refuge from abuse only to return a few days later because we had nowhere else to go started all over again. The song of her life was on repeat. The only difference was now I was big enough not to have to play it over and over with her. I was old enough to do something about it. She could live this way, but I was beginning to realize that I didn't have to.

I refused to go with Mom to a shelter, so when we had to leave the house, I would leave her and Joel to find their own place, and I would stay with a friend. They usually ended up in her car for a couple nights at a time. Thankfully, by this point, I had my own car, which I had bought with money I had earned bussing tables at a local Flying Bridge restaurant. I paid three hundred dollars for a 1988 Ford Escort. I paid for my gas and insurance, and once those were covered for the month, Mom took the leftover money I had. Once I had a car, it never really bothered me that she took my hard-earned money, because with a car, I always had a means to escape when things got bad. I was no longer stuck.

What I didn't have figured out was how to help Joel escape. He was just a little boy taking all of this in, and I felt sick with guilt leaving him in the mess of Mom's choices while I went to stay with a friend. But my mom refused to let me take him when she felt like I was bailing on her. Joel was often her leverage and assurance that I would return when she got things "under control." I regret this at times, but I didn't have it in me to stay with her in those uncertain times just for him. I just couldn't do it. But I always felt like I was rejecting him in those moments. I left him in her mess time and time again. I wonder if Joel felt as rejected by me as I felt by my mom. Rejection stings most when it comes from those you love most.

One night, Mom and Geoff were in an "on again" phase, so we were back to living in the nice house. I walked into the house after work through the garage entrance. As soon as I stepped onto the beige-colored tile of the kitchen floor, I could hear yelling coming from the living room. The kind of yelling that comes from a scared woman, not an angry one. She was clearly afraid and was screaming for help. As soon as I rounded the corner from the kitchen, I saw Geoff shoving my mom up against the sliding glass door that led to a screened-in porch. As he was shoving her against the door, vertical blinds were crashing into each other and falling to the ground. Mom was unsuccessfully batting at him and screaming for him to leave her alone.

Rejection stings most when it comes from those you love most.

That was it. I had had enough. I was so tired of this cycle. I was so tired of mean men. The anger just began to pour out of me, and for the first time ever, I stood up to one of Mom's abusers. I grabbed Geoff by the shoulders, spun him around, and after a few choice words for my new "stepfather," started swinging at him. My shots were about as successful as my mom's had been. I guess I hadn't really progressed in this area since my fight with Alejandro years ago. Nothing landed as I took one bad shot after another. I realize, looking back, that it's a good thing I eventually learned a new way of expressing my anger. I clearly was not a fighter. But there was no going back. At this point, Geoff and I were throwing each other around the living room, and it was becoming increasingly apparent that my fighting record was about to be 0 for 2 as I absorbed another one of Geoff's punches.

I honestly cannot remember how the fight ended. I assume with my mom begging us to stop. But what I do remember is one of the greatest moments of rejection in my life. This moment hurt me deeper than my father walking away and leaving us. Worse than being the smelly kid at school who other kids didn't want anything to do with. There we were, Mom, Geoff, and I, just standing in the living room looking at our wreckage of toppled lamps, strewn papers, and kicked over beer cans. We were standing there looking at the mess and wondering what was next when a string of expletives poured out of Geoff's mouth. They were said to my mom, but they were directed at me. How much of a troublemaker I was, how much I couldn't mind my own business, how he would never let me set foot in his house again, and how she was going to have to choose between him and her son. On and on he went. And I was anticipating my mom putting Geoff in his place, telling him it was one thing to touch her, but it was a whole other thing to touch her son. I thought like many times before when he had hit her that we would pack up and leave. Except this time I thought we'd finally leave for good. Surely, I reasoned, if we leave every time he hits her, we are out of here for good when he hits her kid. I was already mapping out what I could quickly pack and calculating how much combined money she and I had. I was ready to rescue my mom and brother . . . to once and for all be done with this loser. I looked at my mom and waited for her to say the words to Geoff, "We are out."

Except my mom didn't do that. Instead, she turned to me and with tears in her eyes simply said, "Chris, you have to go. You are out."

She threw me out. I couldn't understand. She had a choice, and she chose him. An abusive man she had met a month ago. Not the one who gave her *all* his leftover earnings. Not the one who had been working since he was fourteen. Not the one who had come home from school alone most days since he was ten and watched his little brother so she could work. Not the one who packed, carried boxes, and unpacked with her every couple of months. She rejected me. I felt cast aside. Unwanted. She chose her *abuser* over me. Rejection swallowed me in that moment. Something in me broke that took decades to put back together.

Of all the things people experience, I think rejection stings the hardest and the longest. It holds its poison in your soul for years to come. It makes you afraid to love again. To be vulnerable with anyone. It makes you retreat into yourself and let the world have only the parts of you that you think are shiny enough for people to love. But they never get the full you. They never get all of you. And when you don't reveal the full you, you never truly feel loved. You cannot fully receive love if you are living in fear of being rejected.

Maybe your story of rejection is different from mine. Maybe it isn't one moment you can point to that broke you, but it's a constant reminder that you aren't included. One you see weekly or even daily on Instagram. Or maybe as a child you felt it every day as you walked into the lunchroom anxious that whatever seat you chose, you'd be asked to give it up for someone of a higher status. Maybe your spouse walked out. Or maybe they stayed, but they stonewall you all day, every day. Maybe your dad has never given you his approval.

Rejection stings. And in today's world of capturing and posting every moment of our lives, I'm learning that rejection is a feeling we must all be acquainted with.

But we aren't alone in this. Jesus himself was a man closely acquainted with rejection. I know Jesus experienced all the same emotions we feel, but I think rejection is one he knew intimately.

He was rejected by his own family. Mark 3:20–21 tells us how Jesus's family responded to his growing following and teachings: "Then Jesus entered a house, and again a crowd gathered, so that he and his disciples were not even able to eat. When his family heard about this, they went to take charge of him, for they said, 'He is out of his mind.'"

He was rejected by his own community.

> Jesus left there and went to his hometown, accompanied by his disciples. When the Sabbath came, he began to teach in the synagogue, and many who heard him were amazed.
>
> "Where did this man get these things?" they asked. "What's this wisdom that has been given him? What are these remarkable miracles he is performing? Isn't this the carpenter? Isn't this Mary's son and the brother of James, Joseph, Judas and Simon? Aren't his sisters here with us?" And they took offense at him.
>
> Jesus said to them, "A prophet is not without honor except in his own town, among his relatives and in his own home." (Mark 6:1–4)

He was rejected by his best friends. "Then all his disciples deserted him and ran away" (Mark 14:50 NLT).

He was rejected by his own Father. "Jesus called out with a loud voice, *'Eloi, Eloi, lema sabachthani?'* which means 'My God, my God, why have you abandoned me?'" (Mark 15:34 NLT).

Jesus knows the pain of rejection. He knows what it feels like for your mom to choose her abuser over you. He knows what it's like to be thought of as not good enough for your job. He knows what it feels like to never be able to please your family. He knows your rejection. He sees it. He cares.

Jesus gave us some great examples of how to deal with rejection, and over the past few years, I have been learning some things that can prevent rejection from stinging quite so much. Here are five things you can do to keep rejection from chipping away at you.

1. *Don't leave your peace.* As Jesus was sending out his followers to teach others about him, he gave them this instruction: "If the home is deserving, let your peace rest on it; if it is not, let your peace return to you" (Matt. 10:13). If your family is deserving, if your place of employment is deserving, if your friend circle is deserving, let your peace rest on them. But if they are not deserving, don't leave your peace in their hands. Here is another way I like to say this: let people go only so deep. Not everyone should get full access to your peace. Not everyone should be able to say something or post something that gets to go deep in you. You have a limited supply of peace. Let it rest only on those deserving of it.

Holly and a few of my closest friends get to go deep. They have earned the right to go deep. Holly loved me when I was nothing, she loves me when I screw up now, and she has proven she will be by my side come hell or high water. She gets to go deep. The guy I am going to lunch with who I know is halfway interested in being friends but fully interested in a business deal doesn't get to go deep.

The tricky thing about today's world is knowing that while everyone might get access to you, they don't get to control how deep their words or actions are allowed to go. You control that.

Maybe for you it's a father you know will never approve of you or a boss who doesn't think you have it in you to make it. I can't tell you that you won't feel the sting of their rejection, but I can tell you that you don't have to let their sting go deep. Don't give them full access. Don't leave your peace in their hands.

2. *Quiet your inner critic.* Rejection magnifies the things about yourself that you don't like. Rejection will attach to your insecurities. *I didn't get invited to that party because I am boring. I didn't get the promotion because I am not smart.* Stop doing that! Rejection hurts enough; don't allow your inner critic to piggyback on the pain.

3. *Don't act!* The pain associated with rejection temporarily lowers our IQ and decreases our decision-making ability. This is precisely why you should *not* send a text or comment on a picture when you are reeling from rejection. Rejection keeps you from thinking clearly. So sleep on it. Run your feelings by a friend whose emotions aren't escalated, and then act. I mean, seriously, do you really want to know why he broke up with you or why you weren't asked to the weekend getaway? Oftentimes the answers do nothing but add insult to injury.

4. *Find your flock.* Do you remember the story of the ugly duckling? It is a story filled with one rejection after another. But in the end, the ugly duckling realizes that he isn't ugly; he is just in the wrong flock. I remember one time Holly's feelings were hurt when she saw a post by a group of couples who were hanging out together one night. She said to me, "Wow. I guess they didn't want us there." I grabbed her phone to take a look, and I immediately started laughing. I said, "Are you serious right now? Come on, Holly, you know you wouldn't have gone even if they had invited you!" She looked at me with fake insult and said, "I know. But that's

beside the point. I still wanted to be invited." Sometimes we want so badly to be accepted by a group of people we really don't even like. The problem is that we will never experience the joy of finding our own flock if we spend all our energy begging to be a part of the wrong one. Find your flock. Enjoy your flock.

5. *Focus on your calling.* Jesus felt more rejection than most of us could ever imagine. He was rejected by his family, by the church leaders, by his best friend, and ultimately by his Father. That's a lot of rejection. But do you know what Jesus did every time he was rejected? Jesus always kept his focus on his purpose. He went right on about his business, his business of healing and teaching those who did accept him. He didn't let people's rejection of him keep him from doing what he was called to do. So keep your eyes on your calling. Rejection *never* changes your calling. There is a world out there that needs you. That would be thrilled to have you at their party. That would love to post a picture with you. You can't love those people well if you are spending all your time nursing the wounds caused by those who didn't want to love you well. So stop. Remember that you are chosen by God. You have been given a great purpose on this earth.

> Rejection *never* changes your calling.

Just a few years ago, Holly and I were in a friend circle we enjoyed, one we wanted to be in and truly valued. But I soon realized that we weren't really that wanted. I will never forget the observation Holly made one night after hanging out with them. She said, "Have you ever realized that everyone in this circle only posts pictures with people who have more followers than they do?" I realized this was a platform circle. It turned out to be a circle of you scratch my back and I'll

scratch yours. There was no real community. There was no
vulnerability that bred transparency. Even after realizing this,
it still hurt to feel unwanted. It still stung.

But since then, Holly and I have found a circle that does
love us. One that loves us on our good days and our bad
days. One that chooses us. None are famous. None have
platforms. Never have we felt so loved. So accepted. We are
slowly learning how to open our arms to true friendship,
friendship that risks rejection. Remember the ones who have
chosen you, and slowly, open your heart again. If you are
having trouble, pray this prayer:

*Jesus, rejection is stinging me right now. It has a hold on
me. It keeps me from being vulnerable with those who
love me. It keeps me from admitting when I am wrong.
It keeps me skeptical of the motives of each person I
meet. I pray that your love and acceptance of me will
heal the sting of rejection from my past. Help me to
remember that you have chosen me. You have called
me by name. You want me. You hold me. You have my
present and my future in your hands, and there isn't a
single part of me that isn't known and loved by you.
You know all of me, and you still love me. Help me to
remember your love when I ache for the love of others.
Help me to remember your belief in me when I crave
for others to believe in me. Help me to remember your
inclusion of me when I feel excluded. And may it be
your love, your belief, and your inclusion of me that
heal the sting of rejection I am feeling right now. In
turn, help me to include others. Help me to never treat
someone as something to be discarded, and forgive me
if I've ever done that. Amen.*

8

His Fingerprints

I saw my dad one time between eighth and twelfth grade. While I didn't see my dad much throughout my childhood, he did randomly bless me along the way. Once he shipped me a car on a huge truck that just showed up in our driveway. I had no idea that you could legitimately mail cars! The car was a candy apple red 1979 Ford Ranchero in mint condition inside and out. I quickly sold my three-hundred-dollar Ford Escort with ground effects and a kickin' spoiler and drove that Ford Ranchero with a 351 Cleveland under the hood like Daddy Warbucks himself had sent it to me. To this day, every time we see an El Camino on the road, Holly loves to tell the kids that their dad drove one of those. I proudly correct her each time and properly educate her that a Ranchero and an El Camino are *not* the same thing. The Ranchero is so much bougier than the El Camino. She laughs that I actually believe this. It goes to show how proud I was of that car my dad sent me. In fact, the day I got that car "in the mail" was one of the best days of my life. As a teen boy, I often wished I knew my dad better, but I sure was happy he helped me out when I needed it.

Besides my graduation day, Dad never visited me in Florida during my high school years. But he did start to pay me a little attention after my two no-hitters my senior year. It felt good to have Dad call a couple of times and ask me how ball was going. I was ranking in the Florida high school top ten, so he was sure I would pick a great Division I college to attend the following year. We talked a lot about this when he called. At the time, I didn't know if my success on the field was making him proud and that's why he wanted to talk to me or if he was genuinely interested in me because I was his son. Honestly, I didn't care. I was just excited to get to talk to him occasionally. I would take whatever I could get.

When the time came for college, I didn't go to a Division I school . . . or a Division II, or a Division III. I followed my friend Jason to college. In high school, I spent many nights at Jason's house. For some reason, his parents were okay with the troubled kid hanging with their son, and they were always kind to me. Jason and I played baseball together. We went to all the same parties, but there was always something different about Jason. He fit in with our friend group, but he also stood out at the same time. He was cool but had a different presence about him. He was invited to all the parties, and he would go, but at the beginning of the night, he would always offer to be the designated driver. No one complained about that. Jason was the responsible one in our friendship. He often talked me off the ledge of some pretty dumb thrill-seeking ideas. If it weren't for Jason, I'd have been in much more trouble in high school. And if it weren't for his parents, I'd have been pretty hungry in the evenings or left without a place to stay when Mom decided she wanted me out for nights at a time. Jason and his entire family were different. I loved when he had me over to his house. Being there made me feel safe and calm. It was on those nights that I was exposed to how family members are supposed to interact with each other and how a home is supposed to feel.

One week during our senior year, Jason told me that he was going to try out for a baseball team at a college the following weekend. The college was about two hours away. I didn't even ask what college it was; I just asked if he would mind if I went with him. I may have begged him to let me go for a weekend away. I told him I'd go and support him and that I'd keep him company on the drive there. Jason and his parents agreed to let me tag along. The following day we drove about ninety miles and pulled onto the campus of a small Christian college. I had never even heard of a Christian college, and I was a little amused that this college appeared to be smaller than our high school. By the end of the weekend, we had both been asked to play baseball for the college.

The fact that my closest and safest friend was going to be attending made me very interested in attending there as well. I spent the weekend asking Jason's parents all kinds of questions and trying to understand what my life would look like if I took this step. Although my dad brought up college when we talked on the phone, I honestly hadn't thought too much about it up until that point. I didn't know anyone personally who had ever gone to college, and it wasn't on my radar. Until that weekend. All of a sudden college seemed like a real possibility, but, undoubtedly, there would be many hurdles, and I was just trying to wrap my head around what those would be. It didn't take but five minutes of peppering Jason's parents with questions for me to realize that finances would be the biggest hurdle. Just as quickly as my interest was piqued, it was shut down, and I put the thought of going to college out of my mind. It wasn't a reality in my world. For Jason, yes, but not for me. People like Jason, with stable families and real jobs, got to go to college. I was not like Jason.

Looking back, I don't know if Jason's parents tipped off the recruiter to my passing interest or what, but during the weekend I was asked to attend a private meeting with an administrator of the college to talk about the possibility of me playing baseball for the school. After Jason's parents dropped me off for the meeting, I was escorted by a college student to a large building with a grand lobby. There were high ceilings, what seemed to me to be marble floors, and ballroom-like steps climbing up both sides of the lobby. Whoa. I had never been in a building that nice. As I walked up the stairs with this overly peppy college student, she asked me a million questions about myself, and I quietly answered each one with a one-word answer. I wanted to tell her, "Please. I cannot answer your questions right now. I'm in awe of this building, I'm trying not to get my hopes up that going to college here could ever be a possibility, I'm nervous as heck to meet with an administrator, and I'll never tell you anything about me and where I come from, so please . . . Just. Stop. Talking." I didn't say that though, and she didn't stop talking. When she realized she was getting little to nothing out of me, she stopped with the questions and began to tell me about the history of the college.

As we took a couple turns down hallways of offices, she explained that I would be meeting with Mr. Johnson and that he was the director of recruitment. Mr. Johnson was sharp looking. He had distinguished salt-and-pepper-colored hair and a confidence that only comes with having been around the block a few times. As soon as I stepped into his office and saw the wall-to-wall books and was met with his glowing confidence, my nervousness got even worse. I started to sweat. I could feel it beginning to dampen the inside of my shirt. I had never done this before. I didn't know anything about colleges. I didn't know how any of this worked. It wasn't long before the sweat traveled from my underarms and the back of my neck to my palms. Then my mouth dried up.

I felt like the little boy under the bridge pretending to be a big boy who actually knew what he was doing. I realized that I really wanted to impress this man because, deep down, I really wanted to go to college. I wanted to be here with my safe friend and for us to keep playing baseball together. I wanted the chance to dream of a different life than what my mom had. I rarely got my hopes up about anything because I had grown exhausted from the disappointment caused when things don't turn out the way you hoped. The best way I had learned to cope was just to quit hoping. But I realized in this office that I was hoping. I was hoping for something bigger and better than anything I had ever dreamed of. And that scared me and made me nervous sweat. I realized this man in front of me held the keys to a better future for me. He never said that, but I knew he did. Despite my nerves, I tried to stand a little taller and do my best to look him in the eye when he asked me questions, two things my uncle had taught me.

Mr. Johnson came out swinging. "Chris, do you know what makes this college different from others?"

I stammered, "I have no clue. I hadn't heard of this college until I pulled onto the campus two days ago." Whoops. Wrong answer.

He took a deep swallow and responded, "People who go here believe in Jesus. Do you believe in Jesus?"

I thought about that and then honestly responded, "If you will pay for my college, I'll believe in whoever you want me to believe in." Maybe it was that line, or maybe it was my great posture and eye contact, I don't know, but somehow, some way, this man decided he liked me and said he would make sure finances weren't an issue for me. He'd make sure my college was paid for. I played it off cool as a cucumber, but I was freaking out inside! I wanted to tell him, "You have no idea! I am going to be the best baseball player you've ever seen here! I am going to make great grades. I got this. I will not let you down! Thank you!" Instead, with eyes filled with tears, I simply said, "Thank you. I want to come here."

The decision was done. Jason and I were going to keep playing ball together, and I was going to a Christian college. This decision would change the course of my life. When I look back, this part of my story is a reminder that, yes, there was a lot of darkness, but there was good as well. The fact that Mr. Johnson upheld his end of the bargain and I never had to worry about finances while in college, the fact that I had a car, the fact that I had a close friend who mostly kept me from doing really stupid things—these were God's fingerprints in my life long before I even knew who he was. When I was lost, he kept coming to me. I had never known someone who didn't care whether I performed or not. Every relationship in my life was about how I performed, even the good ones. My coaches expected me to play well, my mom needed me to help provide, my dad called when I succeeded.

It was all I knew. But now, I look back and see a God who kept coming to me when I was doing nothing (but probably causing a lot of trouble) for him. I am overwhelmed by the details he orchestrated in my life long before I knew him. I now can see his fingerprints in my story all along. He made a way for me with that college scholarship.

That's the neat thing about fingerprints. With everything we touch, they are being left behind. On every doorknob, in every bathroom, on our belongings, on those who come into contact with us. But fingerprints are visible only when we look for them. When we study past events. When we slow down enough and are intentional to examine those past events. Then we can see who was there and what they touched. The same is true with God. He's been in your story all along. Though you won't always see him in the moment, in real time as things are unfolding, if you take the time to look back and examine your story, you will see his fingerprints all over it. He was there. Before you even knew who he was, he was working in your story. He was making a way for you.

> He's been in your story all along. Though you won't always see him in the moment, in real time as things are unfolding, if you take the time to look back and examine your story, you will see his fingerprints all over it.

Maybe you are in a season when you can't see God working right now. Things feel hopeless; the worst-case scenario feels inevitable. Maybe the future spouse you always dreamed of doesn't seem to exist and you feel like time is running out. Or maybe the economy is making finding a job in your line of work seem virtually impossible. Maybe despite how many times you've asked God for a friend you can be real with, the hope of finding one is fading.

Let's do a little exercise together. Set aside your current struggle for just a moment and think about your last struggle. What was that one like? The one prior to the one you are currently in. The one that rivaled what you are going through right now in terms of pain and stress. Identify that struggle. Now spend just a couple minutes thinking about the struggle you just identified. First off, I want to congratulate you because you made it through! You. Made. It. You are still here; you are still learning and growing.

Now ask yourself, "How did God work in that situation? Where can I look back and see his fingerprints?" Make a list of all the ways you saw God show up. All the ways you thought maybe he was punishing you at the time but now you can see he was protecting you. Or maybe you felt like you were failing at something, but you were actually finding freedom. Find his fingerprints in your past because doing so will help you hold on to the hope that he is working in your present. He sees your situation today. He cares. He is working. And one day soon you will look back and see his fingerprints in your present struggle as well. You will see how a friend called at just the right time, or how a neighbor dropped off some supplies before you even realized you were going to need them, or how someone placed flowers on your desk at work with a simple reminder that you are not forgotten during a time you felt like God had given up on you.

We need to get better at examining our past for God's fingerprints so that we don't give up hope in our present. Your past will assure you that you have not been abandoned by him. He is still working. He still favors you. He is still here.

9

He Is the Father to the Fatherless

My dad's interest in me left as quickly as it came when he found out I wasn't going to a big college. So, I guess the pride associated with those no-hitters and a possible Division I college had worn off. That's the hard thing about people who are in your life for what you can do. You always have to be achieving more to keep them interested. And every time you achieve a new accolade, you secretly hope that this will be the time they are proud enough of you to stick with the relationship. I wanted that so desperately from my dad. I wanted him to show up and teach me all the things I desperately needed to know at that time in my life. Like how to open a bank account, how to budget my money, how to change a flat tire, how to change the oil in my car. But again, it didn't happen. So I just stuffed all those hopes back down and convinced myself that I didn't care. I was used to him not being involved, and I would just

consider it a bonus when he did care. That was my percep-
tion of fathering. Make money and share it when you feel
like it. Care occasionally. Care when your kids deserve for
you to care.

I had no idea what it meant to be at college, especially a
Christian one. I found out later that Christian college means
a lot of things, but one of the main things is that it has tighter
rules than other colleges. There are curfews and things you
aren't allowed to do. You have to clean your room and show
up to class and not party. I had never in my life had a curfew
or many rules for that matter. But I wasn't worried. I just
thought of college as being like going to military school.
How bad could it be? I'd catch on quickly, or so I thought.

I almost got kicked out several times during my first semester, once for toilet papering the campus with a couple of
guys I barely knew. I know that sounds so cheesy now, but it
was the nineties, and toilet papering was a big thing then. My
baseball coach met me as I was leaving the dean's office after
being told I was on the last straw; one more misstep and I'd
be packing my bags and heading home. Coach got an inch
from my face and quietly yet forcefully stated through his
clenched jaw, "Chris, you are sticking with me from here on
out. If I go to the cafeteria, you go to the cafeteria. If I go to
my office, you go to my office. If I go to the bathroom, you
go to the bathroom." I basically spent my entire first year
of college holding on to the belt loop of my baseball coach,
trying my darnedest not to get expelled.

Between the disappointment of Dad's interest in me fading again and striving to be good so I could last at college, I
began to discover this Jesus everyone seemed to talk about so
much. I liked what the coaches and teachers told me he was
about. I liked that they said I didn't have to try so hard with

him. I felt comforted when they explained that he knew all the darkest parts of my past—parts I never would have put down on paper—and was still interested in me. I liked that although this place was loaded with rules, Jesus seemed to be pretty cool. He wasn't afraid of people who had some dark parts they were trying to hide. I began to take small steps toward this God by simply opening up my mind to the possibility of his existence. Every time I took a step and opened my mind just a little more, I felt better inside. Less angst, more peace. Less striving, more acceptance. Less dark inside, more hope for a better future. Less longing, more satisfaction.

It wasn't long before I hunted down an upperclassman and asked him what being a Christian really meant. Everything he explained, I wanted. I wanted to trade my darkness for God's light in my life. I wanted guidance from someone much bigger than me. I realized as he spoke that everything I was longing for in my earthly father, Jesus was. He was interested. He showed up. He stayed. He chose me. I longed so deeply for my dad to be these things, but he just wasn't. He was never going to be. But Jesus was. Jesus was who I needed most. I needed Jesus more than I needed my dad.

After that early-morning conversation with the upperclassman, I had an opportunity during our daily campus chapel to go forward to the speaking platform and let the faculty know that I wanted to fully accept Jesus as my Savior and Lord. I gave my heart to Jesus. I told him, "I don't understand all of this, but I understand enough to know that you are God and that I need you in my life." I asked him to simply teach me the rest as we went.

Jesus became the Father I longed for. And not just some pie-in-the-sky dad who keeps the world spinning. He started filling gaps in my life that my earthly dad had left. He brought great men into my life to fill them. You know the coach who kept me glued to his side so I wouldn't get expelled from school? He taught me so much during that year at his hip.

Jesus became the Father I longed for.

He had a daughter my age, and he taught me how to speak to a young lady just by the way he was with her. He taught me how to eat dinner at a dinner table with a real family and how to walk away and take a deep breath when anger was boiling over inside. God also filled some gaps through Mr. Johnson. He helped me open my first bank account and taught me how to write a check and balance my account each month. He cosigned on a car for me when my 1979 Ranchero died.

God knew the gaps I had. I had felt those gaps for so long, and my heavenly Father began to fill them. Being his child was what I needed all along. Psalm 68:5–6 says, "Father to the fatherless, defender of widows—this is God, whose dwelling is holy. God places the lonely in families" (NLT). My soul began to settle in that. My angst was still there, but there were times when it left completely. Things were shifting inside and out, and I credit it all to Jesus.

Recently, I was speaking at a conference. I shared just a bit of my story that I have shared in this book, and at times throughout my talk, I used funny examples about my three kids to make a few points. Once my session was over, the conference host dismissed everyone for a short break. I wandered into the lobby to use the restroom and meet a few guests. I exchanged pleasantries with several people, but one young man came up to me and wanted to go a little deeper than the "Nice to meet you. I enjoyed your talk" basics. He looked me square in the eye and asked this question: "How do you know how to be a good father when you didn't have one?" I was not exactly sure what he meant by that, but in my mind, I translated it as this: "I'm surprised that you're a good father. How did you learn to be a good father without one?"

I tried not to feel offended and instead really thought about the question. It didn't take me long to realize that my answer was simple: the very fact that I didn't have a good father made it pretty simple for me to figure out how to be a good one myself. My dad gave me all the material I needed. When my kids are asking for something or going through something, I mentally ask myself this question every time: "What do I wish I would have had in this scenario?" And then I simply try to be that. I've been doing this for sixteen years now.

- When my son was a toddler and playing with his toy cars, I would watch him and tell myself, *I'm sure I would have loved an adult to ask me which ones are my favorite and then teach me how to line them up from my least favorite to most favorite.* And then I would get on the floor and do that.
- If one of my boys asks me to throw a ball, I tell myself, *I would have loved to have a father throw a ball with me and not have to find a brick wall to bounce the ball off.* And then I tell my son, "Sure, I'll throw."
- If my daughter wants to go out to eat, I tell myself, *I would have loved to have a dad I felt comfortable enough to have dinner alone with*, so I respond, "Where are we going, sweetie?"
- If one of my kids needs to stay up late to talk to someone, I tell myself, *I would have loved to have*

someone to talk to who didn't care how many points I scored in the game. I may have to glue my eyelids open, but I'm staying up.

- If my kid is scared and wants me to hang around until they are comfortable, you better believe I'm staying until they feel safe.
- If my boy is in trouble and needs me to bail him out, I am there to bail him out.

Sometimes this goes against the parenting advice that you should let your kids learn from their mistakes. Don't always bail them out or they won't learn to take personal responsibility. Holly and I talk about this a lot, since she leans more to that side, but I simply say that I will find another way to teach my kids responsibility than not showing up when they need me. First and foremost, I want my kids to know they have a loving father who shows up. The rest is all secondary.

Do you know this side of Jesus? There is a tenderness in our heavenly Father that I fear many of us never get to know. He is the one who met the woman at the well and spoke with her in the middle of all her messiness. He spoke with her despite the fact that no one else in society would ever be caught speaking to her. He is the one who bent down and told the disciples to step back so he could look the children in the eye and let them climb all over him. He is the one who made sure his mom was taken care of as he hung in agony on the cross. He is the one who made a point to show Peter that he still loved him even after Peter had completely dissed him. He is the one who provided wine for the embarrassed family who had run out. He is kind. He is thoughtful. He is tender. He is your Father. Galatians 4:6–7 tells us, "Because you are his sons, God sent the Spirit of his Son into our hearts, the Spirit who calls out, '*Abba*, Father.' So you are no longer a slave, but God's child; and since you are his child, God has made you also an heir."

Sometimes we grow up getting to know Jesus as a just God, an almighty God, and he is these things. He is an all-powerful, all-knowing, everywhere-at-one-time God, but he is also a loving and tender Father. He wants you to pull up a chair and tell him all the ways you messed up so he can reassure you that it will be okay. That he can make it all okay. That he still loves you. That he will bail you out of the consequences you deserve because he is your Father, and he can pull strings for you. He can make a way simply because he favors you. This is your God.

> There is a tenderness in our heavenly Father that I fear many of us never get to know.

You may have heard that God loves you, but it may seem like a nebulous thought. There can be a giant chasm between what we know in our minds and what we feel and experience in our lives. Your Father longs to be closer to you than anyone else in your life. You just have to receive him as your Father and allow him to love you and have a relationship with you. Experiencing your Father's love and acceptance is crucial to having a fulfilling life. If you aren't experiencing this gift right now in your life, I encourage you to take two vital steps.

1. *Get in position.* Luke 15:11–32 contains a very compelling story about a prodigal son. This story is a parable Jesus told to illustrate God's unmatched love for each and every one of us. In the story, the son makes some really bad choices and finally comes to his senses after experiencing extreme poverty and humiliation. When he finally admits his

rebellion, he says, "I will set out and go back to my father and say to him: Father, I have sinned against heaven and against you. I am no longer worthy to be called your son; make me like one of your hired servants" (vv. 18–19).

What we see in this part of the story is the son getting in position to receive his father's love. He is in a humble position to receive. Many of us have a tough time receiving the love of the Father because we are not physically positioned in a way of surrender to his fatherhood authority by bowing, bending our knee in prayer, or raising our arms and hearts toward heaven. This is why authentic worship is so important in our lives. When we worship, we are positioning our bodies and our hearts to receive his love. Sometimes it's important to position ourselves and worship even before we actually *feel* his love. Hebrews 11:6 says, "Without faith it is impossible to please God, because anyone who comes to him must believe that he exists and that he rewards those who earnestly seek him."

How are you positioning yourself to receive your Father's love? Remember, he draws near as we draw near to him (James 4:8). I think of the times over the years when my children have had their arms positioned out or up toward me in an intentional posture, communicating the message, "Draw near to me." When they did that, it made me want to reach down and lovingly pick them up. The same is true with our loving Father. He delights when he sees that posture from us, just as fathers and mothers do.

2. *Give love.* Just like we shouldn't wait until we feel like worshiping to worship, we also shouldn't wait until we feel like giving love to give love to others and to the Father. Don't wait around to feel the love of the Father. Give the love away that he has already put inside you. Once you are obedient

to his command to love others, your own experience of the Father's love will grow within you. God does not want you to bottle up his love. The flowing of his love through you to others will bring an incredible blessing to your life. You will begin experiencing the Father's love in a real and fulfilling way. And for those of you who thirst for an "Attaboy" or an "Attagirl" from a father figure, you will get the ultimate "I'm proud of you" delivered to your soul as your actions line up with your life's purpose: to bring God glory with your life by loving him and loving his children around you.

10

Defeating Depression

While things finally felt like they were moving in the right direction for me, they were moving in the wrong direction for Mom and Joel. Mom kept sinking further into the hole of addiction. I don't know if she was struggling with adjusting to me being gone, if she didn't like not having my little bit of financial support, or if there was something else I was unaware of, but her drinking kept getting worse. She would drink until she passed out every night. Then as soon as she'd get up the next morning, she'd start drinking again. It wasn't uncommon for her to have a seizure here and there. My brother was probably nine or ten at the time, and he knew exactly what to do when she started seizing. He'd quickly shove a spoon into her mouth, roll her on her side, and then sit next to her and time the seizures. He knew exactly when they were getting to the "dangerous zone" and he needed to call 911. It made me angry that he had this process down pat. No kid should have to be responsible for that.

But Joel was. I was consumed with guilt for leaving him alone in that environment, but baseball and college were my only way out of the life I knew. I was glad I stayed closer to home for college because even though I wasn't there all the time, I could be home within two hours if Joel really needed me. Sometimes I would drive down on Friday night, pick him up, and take him back to college with me for the weekend. I got to be a pro at hiding him in our dorm. Many of the other guys were in on it, so they would help me keep him hidden. One time Mom called me at school and told me that she didn't have a place for her and Joel to stay for the next few nights. I told her that she had to figure herself out, but I was coming to get Joel. I picked him up and hid him in my dorm room for over a week. We never got caught, and my mom was able to secure housing while he was with me. My brother and I still laugh that we were able to pull that off for an entire week, especially when I was already under close watch from every administrator for my "behavior" issues.

I brought Joel back, and when I did, I discovered how my mom had been able to secure housing. This was one of those moments when all the anger I had regarding her drinking faded away and I began to understand the kind of things she was numbing herself from. Mom had secured a roof over their heads by offering herself to men. Had she always done this, and I was just too young to put two and two together, or was this a new level of desperation for her? I still don't know the answer. I was reminded once again that poverty will cause you to do things you would never do otherwise. I also knew deep inside that those of us who live with someone who struggles with addiction will spend our lives waffling between anger and guilt, between frustration and compassion.

When I realized that day the lengths to which my mom went to put a roof over our heads, the compassion and guilt began to beat out the anger and frustration I had toward her. I had always known this, but that day solidified in me the belief that just because someone is an addict, that doesn't make them a bad person. Oftentimes they are a good person, or a great person for that matter, but for whatever reason, they lacked the opportunities most of us take for granted. Whether the addiction or the lack of opportunity came first is different for all, but I began to form a new thinking that day, one that I tell myself almost daily now. Good people can have some really dark parts to them. Why they have the dark parts or how those dark parts got there varies, but the dark parts don't negate the fact that other parts of them are really good. Sometimes people just need us to believe in the good in them until they can begin to believe for themselves that good still exists. Mom was my hero, and as I scanned the room she was "renting" for her and Joel, I felt tortured with guilt for being hard on her. Sure, she wasn't perfect, but she never beat us, she never left us, and she gave *everything*, including her body, to provide for us. After that day, I realized why her world was dark and depressing.

> Sometimes people just need us to believe in the good in them until they can begin to believe for themselves that good still exists.

And depressed she was. I'll never forget the college baseball game when I saw firsthand how low my mom had gotten. It was a home game, and I was pitching. Holly, my new girlfriend at the time, was in the stands cheering with a group of college friends. The game was in the fourth inning when two police cars pulled up behind the backstop. They had their blue

lights on but no sirens. The second I saw their lights flash-
ing, my stomach sank. I scrolled through everything I could
have possibly done to make sure they weren't coming for me.
I couldn't think of anything, but I was convinced I was the
one they wanted. The officers drove as close to the infield as
they could, paying no attention to the fact that the parking
lot ended two hundred yards behind them. The umpire called
time-out as both cops got out of their cars. They approached
the infield and walked over to my coach in the dugout. They
whispered in his ear for a few moments, and then the cops
and my coach began walking toward the pitching mound. *Oh
no, it's happening. I did something. They're coming to get me.*

They did come for me, but it was worse than I imagined.
My brother had come home from school earlier that day to
find my mom in a bathtub full of bloody water. Mom had
slit her wrists. She was passed out but still alive when my
brother found her. Since her condition was not looking good,
the cops escorted me immediately to the hospital, which was
about ninety miles south of where I was playing. After a long
touch-and-go night, we learned that Mom was going to survive. Joel collapsed in my arms with relief and a flood of tears
when we heard the news. It was in that moment that I began
to wonder if Joel could survive this. I felt so much guilt for
doing whatever I could to make a better life for myself. Joel
was being left behind to deal with everything, and he didn't
deserve this. He was too young to handle seizures, suicide
attempts, and poverty.

I didn't want to go back to that life full-time. But how do
you move on and leave the innocent ones behind? Or how do
you move on and carry the innocent ones with you?

I once heard a lifeguard explain what he had learned in a
continuing education class about water safety. He told me

that you can't rescue someone else when you yourself can barely survive. You have to be healthy and stronger than the drowning victim. If you aren't, you have to get to safety yourself and trust that a stronger lifeguard will be there to rescue them. While that sounds smart to me for water safety, what do you do in real life when there isn't a stronger lifeguard? When, in fact, there is no one else to do the rescuing and you know it? And you love the victim? The victim is the only other person who knows what has lurked behind the door of your home for years. The victim depends on you and needs you to be the rescuer. How do you walk away without at least trying? How do you choose not to fight for them too? This was the turmoil I was in. Joel was drowning, and I didn't know how to save him. I didn't know how to rescue him. And he was the innocent one.

While I didn't want to go back to my old life in any way, and I certainly didn't have the answers for how to fix things for Joel, I did make an agreement with myself that day: I would not leave people to drown. I'd rather die attempting to rescue them than get myself out alive. I am convinced that we all have to come to our own "right" answer on things like this . . . and I am convinced that there is no perfect answer. Just the one that we will be okay to live with for the rest of our lives. That was the answer I could accept. Mom could make her own choices, but I wouldn't leave Joel alone.

I didn't know how to help Joel at that time, and I made a lot of mistakes trying to rescue him. In some ways, I may have actually made things worse for him. But I never lost my heart to help those who are in a situation they didn't choose, especially when it leads them to a deep depression.

A couple of years ago, my friend's wife told him she was leaving him. She was not interested in counseling or trying to salvage things in any way. She was done. He went into some dark days. As his friend, I was unsure how to help him, but I knew he was in a low place. A very low place. I was worried about him and unsure what to do. There was no way to fix his situation. Barring a miracle from God, his wife was not coming home. I had no idea what I could do to relieve his pain. I knew deep down there was nothing I could do but simply support him through it. Depression is dark, and I knew he was in the throes of it.

I went with him to court the day the divorce was to be finalized. I knew no one should have to go through that alone. As we pulled into the parking lot of the courthouse, this grown man just broke down in the car. He collapsed in tears. He was broken. I sat there with my hand on his back and just let him cry. I had no words to make the situation better, no solution to make the pain go away, no life plan to help him get back all he had lost. Sometimes as friends we don't have a single answer, but we can show up. We can be there. We can sit with someone in their pain with a simple hand on their back. It's been several years since that low point for my friend, but I still try to talk to him weekly and make sure he is doing okay. I know what it's like to be in a situation you didn't choose. To not have the right answers. To feel helpless as to what step to take next. To feel as if depression is going to swallow you whole. My friend didn't deserve to go through that painful experience alone, and I wasn't about to let him.

Maybe the darkness of this world or the troubles in your own personal world make you want to curl up and hide under

> Sometimes as friends we don't have a single answer, but we can show up. We can be there.

118

the covers of your bed. One of my friends told me the other day, "I'm not getting out of bed until around nine o'clock in the morning every day because I just can't find a reason to get up earlier." I'm not a counselor, so I don't want to presume that I know how to fight depression and win each time. But I do know from personal experience that depression is tough, and so I have developed some tools to help me when I feel like it's lurking like a dark cloud over my soul.

1. *Get around people.* Depression thrives in isolation. Stay alone, and you will stay depressed. Even when you don't feel like it, push yourself to be with others. Even if it is just one friend you trust. It just takes one friend. One friend who can handle your depression. Who can sit with you in silence if that's all you can do today. If you can't get out of bed, call someone who can pray over you as you lie in bed.

2. *Get professional help.* Our brains can get sick like any other part of our bodies. God has given doctors the knowledge and the schooling to help you with these things. A doctor may have the answer to your healing that you have been praying for. A counselor can give you tools to use daily to get you headed in the right direction in your thought life and motivation. Small wins found through implementing the right tools can lead to big outcomes in the right direction. Whether from a medical doctor or a counselor, get professional help if you are battling depression on a daily basis.

3. *Get in God's Word.* I love the Psalms when depression is knocking on my door. They remind me over

and over of God's love for me. That he has not left me. My mother-in-law taught me a great way to read the Psalms. Start with a simple prayer: "God, teach me something that I need for today." Then open the Psalms to the chapter that corresponds with the day of the month. So, if it's the twenty-third of the month, go to Psalm 23. Read it. Write down anything you learn from it. If nothing speaks to you, add thirty and go to Psalm 53. If nothing, add thirty more: Psalm 83. Still nothing? Read Psalm 113. Then finally Psalm 143. Read each chapter and don't stop until you know that God has spoken something to you specifically. If you get through all five and hear nothing from God, then pray again and start over at the first one you started with that day. He will speak to you. His love will wash over you.

4. *Get caught up in worship music.* Fill your head with something other than your burdens. Fill your head with reminders of God's goodness to you. His care for you. His faithfulness. Get that music playing as soon as your feet hit the floor, and don't stop until your spirits begin to lift.

Depression will not have the last word in your story. It is something you are going through, but it is not who you are. Put these simple tools in place and begin to see God's light drown out depression's darkness.

11

Fewer Victims, More Heroes

The rest of my college years were filled with equal parts peace and turbulence. I loved college. I was known for three things in our small school: I was the captain of the baseball team. I could eat more than any other student. I was moody.

While I had given my life to Jesus, and he was certainly working to shift things inside me, I still had an internal war going on many days. This war kept me from making many friends, but I did have a roommate named Bill who handled my mood swings exceptionally well. We met the first day of college, and as we were both unpacking our things in our dorm room, he tried to make small talk. The more he talked, the more irritated I got. I really didn't want a roommate who was going to probe about my life. I wanted to stay quiet and just let my performance on the baseball field do all the talking. I could tell this private college was filled with rich kids from perfect families, and I was going to keep quiet so no one would pick up on the fact that I wasn't one of them. I knew I did not belong there, but I didn't want anyone else to know that. But Bill just kept on talking. Where are you from? Do you have siblings? Are your parents still here to see your room once you get it set up? Do you want to bring them in now and introduce us? Do you think it would be fun to go to each other's house one weekend and see where we each live?

He was ticking me off. I did not want to chat, and I definitely would never take him home for a weekend. I had no home to take him to anyway. My mom was renting a room that she and my brother were sharing, and that was on a week-to-week basis. I knew there was no way we'd ever be doing a boys' night out. When I just couldn't take one more question from him, I got in his face and angrily grunted, "Dude, you have no clue what I've been through!"

He looked at me, calmly took a step back, and replied, "Well, nice to meet you too, Chris Brown."

From then on, each time my mood got dark or my anger flared, he'd say, "Let me guess. I have no clue what you've been through?" Bill wouldn't let me get away with acting out just because I was in inner turmoil. Bill has no idea how much he taught me during our four years together. Every time he calmly challenged me by repeating my own line, what I really heard in my head was, "How long are you going to be the victim? How is being a victim working out for you?" Bill was teaching me that I had a decision to make: Was I going to play the victim card with my one life?

I had a decision to make: Was I going to play the victim card with my one life?

Not only was Bill teaching me some really big things, but he was also a social butterfly. He was into dating and dating a lot. And he always made sure I was set up for a weekend date as well. During the next four years, Bill set me up on countless blind dates. Most of the time he'd tell me about a date he had set me up on about an hour before we would have to leave. I acted like he was killing me, but, honestly, I appreciated all the legwork he did. I was shy, and it was much easier to let Bill do the asking for me.

I dated a few girls in college, but the only thing I was serious about was baseball. That is, until I met Holly my junior year. We still argue over the way we first met. She swears her roommate told her I called her dorm room and asked to talk to her. I did not do that. But she says even if it wasn't me, someone told her it was, and she always believed I was interested in her from that night on. That's the story she sticks with to this day.

I know that never happened. This is how I remember it. She approached me after a volleyball game in the gymnasium one night and simply introduced herself to me. I acted like I had never seen her before, but I had. I knew who she was. We talked a few times after that, and I was getting very close to asking her out, but things kept getting in the way: work, baseball practice, but mostly Bill and his double dates. You see, by this point, Bill and I had been roommates for three years, and he was used to setting me up each weekend. I admit that I hadn't told Bill I had my eye on a girl and was thinking of asking her out on my own.

My failure to give Bill a heads-up is exactly where I went wrong. One Friday night, Holly and I were hanging out on campus, and I was ready to ask her out. I mean, it was obvious to both of us that we were into each other and that it was long past time for me to ask her on a date. I was so close as we stood under the gymnasium portico, but no joke, as we were flirting and talking, Bill drove up in his car, threw open the passenger door, and without a second glance at Holly said to me, "Hop in. I've got a hot girl in here you're taking out tonight." I did what any other college boy would do. I hopped in . . . no questions asked. That didn't go over so well with Holly. Like I said, I was shy, and she was *not*. She let me know that she wasn't impressed and that she had plenty of others interested in her, so we went our separate ways before things ever got started between us.

Through the disappointment of things not getting off on the right foot with Holly, through the equal parts wonderful and miserable blind dates, through all the baseball practices, overtime hours, and late-night studying, Bill was a steady friend. His steadiness gave him a voice in my life, and he helped me change the narrative that played on repeat in my head. He subtly taught me that I had a choice: I could be the victim in my story, or I could be the hero. Yes, no one knew what I'd been through. But that didn't have to hurt me. It could be my greatest asset in a new setting like college. No one knew my baggage. No one knew that I wasn't just like all the other kids at a private college: rich and from good, healthy families. No one knew that I was different, and so therefore no one treated me like I was a lesser version of everyone else there. And consequently, no one was going to give me special treatment because they felt sorry for me. The playing field had been leveled for me. I now had the opportunity to succeed just like everyone else.

And I did succeed thanks to Bill and many mentors in my life. I became the treasurer of the student body, I graduated with a degree in business administration, and I was eventually inducted into my college's Hall of Fame for baseball. I liked being the hero better. It was working for me. People looked at me differently . . . they respected me. For the first time, people weren't snubbing their noses at me or feeling sorry for me. I walked into college a victim, but Bill taught me that being a hero is a much better role to play.

What role are you playing in your story: the victim or the hero? I am not at all minimizing what was done to you or excusing anyone else's actions, but I am taking away their ability to define you. You don't have to be their victim. You can be the hero. The one who overcame. The one who succeeded despite what they did to you. The one who gave all that pain to God and let him make something beautiful with it.

> **What role are you playing in your story: the victim or the hero?**

In the Bible, Joseph's eleven brothers abused him and sold him to slave owners who took him to Egypt. They gave up on him. They abandoned him. He was the victim, and he had every right to live like a victim. But he didn't. Instead, he decided at every turn that he was not going to be the victim. He was going to make the best of each and every situation he found himself in. He was going to be the hero. And he was. He was the hero for his friends, for his boss, and for his country. And crazy as it seems, the day eventually came when he was the hero for his brothers. The same brothers who wanted to be rid of him and sold him to strangers.

Several years after selling Joseph into slavery, the brothers were starving because there was a famine in their country and they had no food. They were at a point where they were going to die if they did not get their hands on some food. So they traveled to Egypt to ask this neighboring country if they could buy some food. Well, guess who was in charge of all the food in the land of Egypt? You guessed it: Joseph. Joseph had succeeded so much in this country he had entered as a foreign slave that he was now the second in command—the vice president of the entire country. Joseph didn't get to that position by sitting and nursing the wounds his brothers had inflicted on him. No, he decided he was going to use every opportunity given to him to make the best of the one life he had. He said no to victim mentality.

When Joseph's brothers realized they were begging before the brother they had sold, they stopped begging for food and instead begged for forgiveness. Joseph's words to his brothers are the words of someone who had determined that it is better to be the hero than the victim. Joseph said, "You intended to harm me, but God intended it all for good. He brought me to this position so I could save the lives of many people" (Gen. 50:20 NLT). You meant to punish me; God was preparing me. You meant to abandon me; God was advancing me. You meant to destroy me; God was developing me.

Not for a moment would I downplay the pain you've been through; I'm just inviting you to join me. Let's be Josephs together. Life is better when we are the hero rather than the victim. Take time to grieve, but do the work and heal, because there is a world that needs you. Just as God did for Joseph and for me, he will take what the enemy meant for evil and use it for good in your life. It will happen. Keep on.

12

The Beauty in Brokenness

While Holly and I got off to a rocky start, I was not going to be deterred. I made a point to keep bumping into her. I liked her. She was pretty, but that wasn't what was so eye-catching about her. It was her confidence, especially for a freshman. I would watch her hold the attention of an entire crowd as they listened to her stories. They would all be belly laughing in a matter of minutes. She had what I didn't. She was wide open. Nothing to hide. She held her head high. There was no shame in this girl. She loved every part of life. There was no depression or angst about her. Her personality was contagious. She was strong. Living a great life seemed doable around her. I loved being around her. So I made a point to do just that.

Holly won't admit it even today, but she is a bit of a nerd, so it didn't take me long to figure out that she spent most afternoons in the library. I had *never* been in the library.

Regardless, I started keeping tabs on her whereabouts, and I "coincidentally" started stopping by the library in the afternoons. On one of our not-so-accidental run-ins in the library, I got up the nerve to ask her on a date. It was a simple date. We had a curfew, and I didn't get off work until late, so we had only about an hour and a half to hang out. Of course, Bill brought along a girl, and we doubled up. Holly and I flirted and laughed all night. I didn't get to know too much about her that night. I just left knowing I wanted to get to know her. Who was this girl?! She was eighteen but had the confidence of a much older woman, but not in an arrogant way. Just in an "I got this" way. I liked her. *A lot.* I asked her out again and again and again. Within a few months, we were pretty serious.

It didn't take long for me to discover that not everything was perfect in Holly's life. Her dad was in his early forties, and he was dying of a brain tumor. Her mom was scared to death. Holly was one of five kids, and while she didn't grow up like I did, money was a big issue for her family, and paying for college was a day-by-day thing in her world. She had received some academic scholarships, but she wasn't on a full ride. Holly was a saver, so with what her parents were able to contribute, her scholarships, and what she had saved up, she had paid for her first semester up front and was working two part-time jobs in hopes of being able to pay for her second semester at this private college. But she told me quite clearly that she would not be coming back after her freshman year.

She would have no money left, and she would not take out a loan. She refused to put that financial pressure on her parents when they had four other kids and her dad was so sick. I asked her one day what she planned to do. She said,

"I hope I know who I am going to marry by the time I leave here. Then I'll just take classes at the community college in my hometown and work until we marry."

This sounded like crazy talk to me. "So, let me get this straight. In one year, you are going to meet the person you're going to marry, *and* he's going to fall in love with you enough to propose?"

She said, "That's the plan, but if it doesn't happen, I'll come up with another plan."

I didn't think too much about it . . . I just really didn't want her to leave.

When finals rolled around, I realized it was about a week before Holly was to leave for the summer. I finally got up the nerve to ask her what our relationship would look like with her leaving for good. She casually let me know that the school had asked if she wanted to work full-time at the college over the summer. Not only would they pay her and let her live in the dorms for free, but she could also take summer classes for free. Holly was all in on that, and I was thrilled because I lived near the college year-round and would get to see her all summer. That was the best summer of my life. We both worked so hard and took classes, but we snuck in a trip to the beach, a walk to the park, or a quick lunch in the cafeteria whenever we had a spare ten minutes. My life quickly revolved around when I could see her again.

My world was painfully broken behind the scenes, but it had always been that way—that was my normal. Her perfect-behind-the-scenes world was crashing in on her. Her dad was losing his memory and his ability to physically function at a young age, and her mom was overwhelmed and scared. Holly was carrying a lot of pain too. It was a bond that we shared. When we were together, we knew that there was so much more to both of us than what anyone else at the college knew. There was a comfort in piece by piece opening up our broken parts to each other. She made me feel normal, and she tells me that I helped her feel safe. Tragedy will bond you like nothing else, and we experienced that in the summer of 1999. By the end of the summer, I was head over heels in love with her. I wanted her to be my wife. We were so young (nineteen and twenty-two), but I didn't care. I proposed, and Holly said yes. But she still stuck to her plan. She left private college and went back home to work, go to community college, and now plan a wedding as well.

> My world was painfully broken behind the scenes, but it had always been that way— that was my normal.

Holly taught me that summer that I was not the only one hurting. I was not the only one broken. She told me later that she fell in love with me because of my brokenness. Because behind what everyone else saw—an athlete and a student body leader—there was a softness. A softness that is only crafted from a heart that knows pain. That knows what it's like to be scared and to put on a brave face. That can see what is really behind the words of another. Such a person can identify pain in someone who has yet to speak a word, someone who is putting on a happy face. People who haven't been through pain don't get that. They don't have those eyes. Holly and I have been married for more than twenty years, and it all started with bonding in our brokenness. Our broken parts began to heal as we opened up and shared with each other the parts that we were hiding from everyone else.

Do you tend to run from relationships and opportunities because of your brokenness? Do you find yourself feeling that if people really knew who you were, they would walk away? We are in awe of people because of their strength, but we connect with people because of their brokenness. Your brokenness allows you to notice the person in the room who feels anxious or undeserving. The person who has battled addiction can recognize and respond appropriately to someone else who is battling. If you've never been broken, you don't see it. You don't see the depth of pain in your friends' eyes or the loneliness of the cashier at a store. Broken people see these things, and they know how to respond in a way that lets others know their pain is seen. Don't despise what broke you; it is exactly what will heal the broken parts of others. There is tremendous beauty in our brokenness.

> Our broken parts began to heal as we opened up and shared with each other the parts that we were hiding from everyone else.

13

Giving Loss Meaning

During my senior year in college, my dad started to call me regularly. I loved it. I respected him because, to me, he had everything I craved: a stable home, a nice car, a job that at least in my eyes made him a lot of money. I was thrilled that he was finally making the effort to get to know me. All those years I had wished so badly that he would just call and ask me how things were going. There were so many times I wanted to tell him we needed help. Mom needed help. He never called. But now, he was calling regularly. In fact, after his first few calls, we scheduled a standing weekly phone call for Sunday nights at 9:00. We would talk about baseball, my studies, Holly, and our future wedding plans. I figured that since I was older and not so much to handle, my dad and I would be close. It felt right inside to be getting to know my dad. That rejected little boy was beginning to feel worthy of his dad's attention. I loved those phone calls and never missed one. No matter what I was doing, at 8:45 p.m., I would hustle back to my room and tell everyone they needed to leave or promise to be quiet because I had an important meeting in a few moments. And then I would sit there on my bed and wait for the phone to ring.

Holly and I were getting married in December, which was just a couple of months away at this point. My dad was planning to come for the wedding. It would be the first time I would see him since the one time I saw him in high school. He asked if he could come a few days early so he could spend some time with me. He explained that he had a big surprise he was planning on giving me. He also told me, "Don't you worry about that honeymoon. You take your wife somewhere wonderful because it's on me." I was so pumped I didn't have to take Holly on a poor man's honeymoon! My dad was bailing me out! And when he said somewhere wonderful, I wasn't thinking Paris or anything. My world was very small back then, but since I lived in Florida, I was thinking maybe a nice cruise or a resort in the Caribbean.

As the wedding date got closer, Dad and I were talking more and more. I was so excited for him to meet Holly. I knew he would be incredibly impressed with her and think that I had clearly outkicked my coverage. I couldn't wait to go golfing together and give him a run for his money. I wanted to ask him well-thought-out questions about being a businessman. So I made a list of all the questions I wanted to ask him about being successful: What is one thing you wish someone had told you about business when you were my age? What has been the number one thing that has contributed to your success? What are bosses looking for from a new, inexperienced employee? I was going to prove to my dad that I was well on my way to becoming a great man. A great businessman. I was going to be like him, and I wanted to make sure he saw that. I had my questions ready, my outfits chosen, and a list of things for us to do together during his visit. I was prepared because, more than anything, I wanted my dad to feel proud of me.

The wedding was set for December 18, 1999. Dad was to arrive on the fourteenth. On November 29, I received an unexpected call from my dad's sister. I barely knew my aunt. I had maybe seen her twice in my life. She sounded nervous and unsteady. I was standing in the kitchen at Holly's parents' house because we were spending Thanksgiving break with her family. Holly has a big family, so things were loud, and I could barely make out what my aunt was saying among all the laughter and sarcasm being tossed around the room. My aunt stopped talking and asked me to go into a quiet room where we could talk privately. I remember stretching the phone cord across the kitchen and into the dining room and shutting the door behind me. I could hear my aunt take a deep breath, and then with a shaky voice, she explained that my dad had had a brain aneurysm at home earlier that night and was now in the hospital on life support. She said it didn't look good and I needed to get to California quickly. She said she'd pay for me to book the first flight I could find. I didn't really know what any of that meant, but when I explained it to Holly's mom, I could tell by her reaction that this was horrible news. She helped me book a flight, and within a couple of hours, I was on my way to California to see my dad. This was before smartphones, so I couldn't do any research to better understand what kind of condition my dad was in. Instead, I slept off and on during the flight and kept wondering what a brain aneurysm even was.

My aunt picked me up at the airport and took me directly to the hospital. We talked very little in the car, but I could tell by her sympathy that things were not looking good. When I walked into his ICU room, Dad didn't look a thing like I remembered him. In fact, I didn't recognize him at all. He was swollen everywhere. Tubes were all over him, and a machine was breathing for him. My dad was strong, though, and he was only forty-five, so I had no doubts he would make it through this. This was just temporary. He'd bounce back. He had to bounce back. We had plans and twenty-two years to catch up on. I had a wedding in a few weeks, and he was going to be there.

I sat by his bed for two days straight. His swelling only got worse, and the nurses seemed to add more tubes every few hours. There was a lot of whispering between the doctor and my aunt. Everyone seemed to look at him with pity in their eyes and then turn and glance at me with the exact same look.

As I sat by that hospital bed, I didn't really know what to say. I mean, I was a man of few words already, and he was unconscious, so words were very few. But I did tell him that I wished we would have spent more time together throughout the years. I told him that I was one semester away from beginning to become a great businessman like him and that I had a lot of questions to ask him when he woke up. I told him that I planned not to be poor anymore. I told him that the day I walked outside and saw the red Ford Ranchero he had shipped to me for my birthday was one of the best days of my life. And then when it was just the two of us in the room, because I was really unsure of myself and I didn't know if I'd be able to answer the questions people might ask me, I explained that I'd chosen to follow Jesus and that he was changing so much for me. I said that when he woke up, I wanted to tell him about Jesus. I wondered out loud if maybe he might like to know a little more about him as well.

I spent every moment I could in that fake leather turquoise recliner waiting for Dad to wake up. I went back to my aunt's house here and there to nap and grab a shower, but that was it. On the third day, several of my aunts and uncles came in the room and encircled the recliner. Kathleen spoke up first. She explained to me that Dad was not going to wake up. He was not going to make it through this. That it was over. He was going to die. I couldn't wrap my head around what she was saying at that moment. I had too much hope that he would finally be a dad to me. Too much excitement about him coming to visit and meet Holly. Too much longing to hear him tell me he was proud of me. It was all too much. But even though my world was spinning and my heart was sinking, my aunt didn't stop talking.

She explained that I was his only child, and since he wasn't married, I had to be the one to decide to pull his life support. I needed to tell the doctor it was time to let him go. *Are you freaking kidding me? I am twenty-two. I just started talking to this man a few months ago, and now you want me to be the one to decide that now is the time he should die? Heck no. I'm not ready for this. I'm not ready to give up on having a father. I'm not ready to face the fact that I will never hear him say he's proud of me. I'm not ready, and I'm definitely not doing that.*

I begged and pleaded. "You guys know him better than I do. You know what he would want. You are all much older than me. I don't want to make this decision. I don't know him that well, and I don't know you guys at all. Please don't make me do this."

My aunt was so kind. She was patient. She told me she'd give me as much time as I needed, but she couldn't take this responsibility away from me. By law, I had to be the one to speak with the doctor. This was way too much for my heart to handle. I had learned to step up and help support my mom, I had learned to ask others to teach me things my dad should have taught me himself, I had learned how to make it without his presence, but to be the one to determine that his time on earth was over? I could not do it. I could not carry the weight of this decision.

But life can be cruel, and so often, it doesn't care what we are or aren't ready for. It was going to force me to make this decision no matter how unprepared I was. I slipped into the bathroom and muffled a few sobs, splashed water on my face, and simply prayed, "Jesus, I need your help. I can't do this." I hid in there for a while and then went and sat by my dad's bed for a few hours and never acknowledged the conversation I had had with my aunts and uncles. I just sat there and stared blankly at this lifeless version of my father. Eventually, I got up the courage to speak with the doctor. He explained to me that even if, and that was a highly unlikely if, Dad got healthy enough to breathe on his own, he would never talk, never eat, never walk, and never be himself ever again. His brain was damaged beyond repair. The man I wanted to know was gone.

I agonized for several more hours. I called Holly. She was nineteen and didn't know what to do either. We got her mom on the phone and asked her for advice. This is what I learned: no one wants to give you advice when it comes to deciding whether or not someone should live. Holly and I prayed to-gether. I didn't like the decision I had to make, but I did feel like it was the best one. I hate when the right decision is the hard decision. Isn't that the way it usually is though? If I am stuck between two choices, I often ask myself, "Which one is harder?" I have learned that the hard decision is most often the right decision. After a few more prayers for strength, I made the hardest decision of my life. I went to the doctor and told him to pull the plug.

My dad never got to meet Holly or see me play college baseball. He didn't make it to the wedding. I never knew the surprise he had for me. Dad was turning our relationship around, but, unfortunately, it was too late.

Holly and I still got married two and a half weeks later. Mom came to the wedding drunk, and Dad was gone. I was grieving the loss of being able to even hope that Dad would show up to some event. I didn't realize how much I missed just being able to hope for his presence or to pretend he was just about to arrive. I'd pretend that he was coming on my birthday right before it was time to eat cake or that he was walking up behind the backstop when I was up to bat. I didn't just lose him . . . I lost getting to hope for him.

At my wedding, five people showed up on the groom's side. Jason's parents, my aunt, her daughter, and my mom. Joel was my best man. Holly and I had to reroute our honeymoon because now it was all on me, and by this point, we all know how poor I was. So we did have to do a poor man's honeymoon. It was probably good that we didn't spend a lot of money on it because I cried the entire time. It was not the honeymoon anyone grows up dreaming about, that's for sure. My excitement for marriage mixed with waves of intense grief for my dad. All the hopes I had just begun to dare to

> I was grieving the loss of being able to even hope that Dad would show up to some event.

dream were dashed as quickly as they came. To say that our honeymoon was bittersweet would be a huge understatement. And then Christmas was just days away, but all of a sudden, things just didn't feel very merry.

I know for others the same is true: when life is hard, holidays have a way of making it even harder. Grief by itself is isolating, but grief when the rest of the world is celebrating feels like it's going to swallow you whole. When we are grieving, we don't want to cut down a live tree, wrap presents, or sing carols. We want to cry. We want to be alone, yet we don't want to be alone. We can't make a decision about which color of hoodie to purchase for our sibling when our heads are filled with the fog of pain and regret. We want anything but what we're facing.

I remember trying to shop for Christmas gifts and feeling panicked inside. I thought, *How in the world can I walk through Target when my dad just died? Look at all these people hustling around, buying gifts, and sipping coffee. And no one—not one person—knows or cares that my dad just died*. I felt sick with guilt and anxiety. Guilt that I was doing seemingly meaningless things like shopping for a present when my dad had just lost his life. When he would never again have the opportunity to go Christmas shopping or sip a Starbucks holiday drink. Guilt that my marriage started with me crying the entire honeymoon. Guilt that I should have waited for a few more days to see if maybe, just maybe, my dad would have woken up normal. I believe that God heals. Maybe I gave up too soon, and he was just about to do a miracle. I felt wrapped in anxiety that the world was moving on without me. My dad wasn't a present father at all, but he did bail us out here and there, and he was the *only* person I knew who would do that. I had no safety net now. I had no one. I was anxious that I now had a wife to provide for and a brother who I was leaving behind in my mom's messes. I was twenty-two, and I was not ready for any of this. Our first week as husband and wife and our first Christmas together were full of pain.

One day during our honeymoon, I stayed by myself all morning and let Holly do her own thing. By the time we met for lunch, I was flooded with guilt over our wrecked honeymoon and grief over the loss of my dad. I felt paralyzed. Then I looked up to find her blue eyes filled with tears. She said, "I'm sorry you're going through this. I'm sorry so many of your hopes and dreams just got crushed at the same time you were expecting to birth new ones. You don't have to say a word the rest of the trip if you don't want to. Don't worry about me."

And in that moment, I was strengthened. I don't think the strength came from her words but from the compassion and grace I felt in her eyes. I realized that God in his grace and timing knew this pain was coming, and he had brought me a companion. Maybe you have a friend or family member you can talk to or, better yet, one you can just be nearby. Or perhaps you can get outside in the beauty of God's creation for a moment of peace. It was that moment with Holly that got me through the holidays that year. While pain is often what shapes us, it's the small slivers of hope that sustain us.

> While pain is often what shapes us, it's the small slivers of hope that sustain us.

Unfortunately, the grieving process cannot be shortened if healing is what you want for yourself. Even when I longed for my grief to subside and give way to a merry Christmas, the pain remained. And I know I'm not alone. As a pastor, I've walked beside many people struggling to make it through the holidays.

Those of you who are hurting deeply, I am so sorry. I understand your pain may not go away anytime soon. I simply pray that in the midst of the pain you find moments of joy when the pressure on your chest lightens, the knot in your throat eases, your anxiety lifts, and hope peeks through. Oh how special it is when not only your mouth smiles but so does your soul.

You may not be able to break away from the grief of loss to sit in the reminder of God's goodness for a whole hour or a whole afternoon, but maybe you can do it just one minute each day. And then after a while, two minutes, and then a few weeks later, three minutes, and then four. Until the frequency increases, your chest begins to find reprieve from the pressure, and the lump in your throat starts to lessen in size. Keep looking for these small glimpses of a better tomorrow. They will be there. You will see the goodness of the Lord again. You will belly laugh again.

You might unexpectedly receive the gift of a few hope-filled hours while gazing at a Christmas tree lighting up a darkened room, or maybe in the kitchen baking cookies with your kids, or in the midst of a great meal and conversation with loved ones. And next year, when you're in a new season, you'll look back and say, "That pain almost did me in, but by God's grace, he gave me the small doses of joy I needed in each season. Those glimpses of joy reminded me of what life could be. It's because of those moments that I survived."

I've come to realize that hope is a confident expectation of a better tomorrow based on the character and promises of God. It's okay to cry and grieve and stay a thousand miles away from Target. Just don't let pain rob you of God's small graces. Keep your heart settled on these hope-filled gifts from the Lord and let them carry you. Today you might have a wave of joy that passes through your grief. Relish it. Smile without guilt. Look your loved one in the eye. Grab a pen and write down what God blessed you with. Make it last as long as you can. And before you know it, it will happen more and more, and your soul will be strengthened. You will know that your heart is healing. The pieces will begin to come back together, and you'll start to be confident once again that you will make it through. But it all starts with finding a single moment in the midst of your deep pain and then fully embracing it, allowing it to sooth your spirit.

Oh, what I wouldn't do to be able to spend a twenty-four-hour day with my dad. Because of loss, I long for what I can't have. I can't go back in time, so how can I make sense of the pain? Holly and I have both lost our earthly fathers, and we have decided to redeem the pain and leverage the horrific reality that they are no longer with us by making an impact that makes them smile from above. Our dads have taught us that life is short and that we get only one chance to make a difference. Because of this, loss has not had the final word. Our impact is getting the final say as we seek to serve and minister to our community.

I am sure that if you are old enough to pick up this book and read it, you have experienced some loss in your life. We've all experienced loss, whether the loss was caused by death, a move to another state, or someone who said "I do" but didn't. Or maybe it was a dream that was lost. I encourage you to focus on how you can redeem that loss for good. Whether the loss in your life was due to foul play or not, I offer Romans 12:21 to you: "Do not be overcome by evil, but overcome evil with good." In this verse, we see our ability to redeem the unfortunate things that happen in our lives. Sometimes the pain is caused by us, and sometimes it's caused by others. Sometimes it's just somehow in God's plan, and we may never find out why. But we definitely have an adversary who seeks to kill, steal, and destroy. The passage of Scripture that helps me the most when it comes to things I believe are a by-product of a very real Satan who likes to bring loss into our lives is Genesis 50:20, which says, "You intended to harm me, but God intended it for good."

I'm convinced that we are called not just to endure loss but to give it meaning. To transform the sting of loss into purpose for today.

14

Past Regret,
Today's Freedom

It was during this time of starting my final year of college, burying my dad, and marrying Holly that I decided I had to find a way to step in and help my mom and Joel more. Yes, addiction was swallowing her day by day, but she had tried hard for us. Before I was old enough to work and help with the income, she had worked two or three jobs. She rescued me when I was stuck in that gang activity. And now, she and Joel were moving from house to house, renting rooms from people that were too often paid for with favors to men. They were also still spending many nights in her 1979 Dodge Diplomat. My mom was not a loose woman. She was desperate, and I wanted—no, I needed—to help her. Mom and Joel still lived in a town ninety miles from my college, and although Holly and I were newlyweds and barely making ends meet, we decided to move Mom and Joel closer. We wanted to do our best to help Mom pay for an apartment so she wouldn't have to do the things she had been doing. And with them being closer, I felt better knowing that if she or Joel needed me, I could be there in a matter of minutes.

Holly was working as a nurse's assistant making eight dollars an hour, and I was working as a financial assistant making seven dollars an hour. We could barely afford to feed ourselves, but they needed help. I found Mom and Joel the cheapest apartment in the area. I don't know why I thought that having my mom ninety miles closer to me but placing her in an apartment building filled with scumbag men, drugs, and addiction would help her in any way. I sincerely wanted to help her, but things just kept getting worse. Someone who struggles with addiction cannot win in an environment like that. It was a recipe for disaster. Mom was raped by a man one afternoon. I knew this man. I had seen him several times when I went to visit, and I knew he was trouble from the moment I saw him, but I never thought for a minute that he was capable of such a thing. I was scared of what I would do if I ever saw this man again. It was God's grace that I never did.

Not only did the move set Mom up for failure, but it also set our relationship with each other up for failure. For the first time in several years, I was seeing her addiction up close again, and as it had when I was growing up, it made anger boil inside me. She had promised that if I moved her closer she would quit drinking and get a steady job waiting tables. She lied.

Joel would often call me crying, telling me Mom wouldn't stop seizing because she was drinking and taking pills. The calls came earlier and earlier with each passing day. I remember once Joel called, afraid she was going to die. He was thirteen at the time. Fuming inside, I left my classes and went to the apartment. The second I walked through the front door,

Joel left my mom's side and ran to give me a hug. Through sobs he said, "I'm so glad you're here to help Mom." As if I had ice in my veins, I looked at Joel and said, "I'm not here to help her. I'm here to help you. Get your things. We're leaving." During all of this, my mom was lying on the floor seizing just five feet away. As I looked at her body shaking uncontrollably and blocking the hallway to the bedrooms, something inside me broke. *I can't do this. Not with her.* I didn't touch her. I didn't check on her. Joel cried harder and begged me to just wait until the ambulance arrived before we left so we would know if she was going to make it or not. I told Joel, "I'm going to pack your bags. Hopefully, they will be here before I'm done, because we aren't waiting." I then proceeded to step over my mom's seizing body and into Joel's room to gather some clothes for him.

This is the life of living with an addicted person. One moment you will give everything you have to rescue them, and the next moment you are giving up on them. Then the overwhelming guilt of giving up on someone you love follows. Addiction takes love and hate, sympathy and apathy, anger and compassion and blends them all together so you never know which one is going to come out or how it will be directed in the next scenario the addict pins you in.

I quickly learned something about those who struggle with addiction: they hurt you. Over and over, they will hurt you. They are often so focused on their own pain that they are clueless or apathetic about the pain they are causing. They need more than they give . . . often for way longer than you are willing to pay. It's angering. It's frustrating. It's exhausting. But you know what I'm learning? There are things in life far worse than being hurt. Like giving up on someone too soon or missing the comeback because I didn't stay for the game or living life shut down because I didn't want to risk being hurt again or failing to give the grace I have so often needed myself.

I don't pretend to be an expert on anything I am writing on these pages. I'm simply trying to help us find some common ground in our sources of pain so that we can move through that pain together into the beauty that I know God has for each of us. Beauty can be found in any story. He makes all things beautiful in his time. It is our time to find some beauty in our past pain.

> He makes all things beautiful in his time. It is our time to find some beauty in our past pain.

I loved my mom, but she hurt me a lot. And my greatest regret, the one that trumps all others, is that I gave up on her. Emotionally, I threw in the towel. I didn't care anymore. She had hurt me enough with her issues, and I wasn't going to feel that hurt anymore. So I quit on her. That regret cuts deeper and causes more pain than any hurt she caused me. I wish I had known some of the things I know now when I still had the chance to love her better.

As a pastor, I find myself looking people in the eye and saying over and over, "If you fall one hundred times, we will be here to help you get back up." I do that because I'm determined; I am not going to quit on people. I understand that this is easier said than done. It's easier to hold on for people you don't know up close and personal than for those who get access to hurt you over and over again. It's messy to walk alongside hurting people, but I don't want a polished life. I want an impactful one. I don't want to distance myself from the mess. I want to live in a way that the most down-and-out friends of mine would say, "Everyone gave up on me *except* this one guy, Chris." "Everyone told me I could never become anything else *except* my friend Chris." "Everyone abandoned me in my darkest hour *except* Chris." At my own risk of being hurt, I want to be the exception. My journey with my mom taught me that I want to stay in people's lives with them. Boundaries, yes. Giving up? Never.

I'll never forget this one woman in our church, Kathy, who attended every week. Kathy was frustrating. She walked into services late, causing disruptions in our small auditorium. She'd beg to be involved only to not show up time and time again. She often needed money and would ask anyone for it. She monopolized a small group. She would love you one moment then hurl insults at you the next. She didn't fit into a neat assimilation system, and, honestly, she took more than she gave back. She was tough . . . and messy. She was a deeply hurt person who at times hurt a lot of us.

Like my mom, Kathy never did overcome her pain and clean up her mess this side of heaven. But despite the frustrations, disruptions, and hurt Kathy caused, our church family kept on with her. We didn't give up on her. And while addiction cut her life short here on earth, you know what I did get to see in Kathy's lifetime? I got to see her decide to follow Jesus and ask me to baptize her. When I baptized Kathy and she came up out of that water, I'll never forget the look of sheer elation on her face. I got to witness a moment of *victory* for someone who lived almost every moment of every day defeated. I saw hope and joy in the eyes of someone who knew the deepest pits of despair. This was her moment, and I knew in that moment that she soaked up how much she was loved by God. I'm so thankful we didn't quit on Kathy.

Kathy died less than a year after getting baptized. Every day, Kathy was a reminder that addiction hurts those you love but that addicts are still worth our time and energy. They need us. They need people to love them like Jesus regardless of their mess. Mom taught me how to love the Kathys in my life better.

Addiction is complex. And the layers upon layers of emotional wounds it causes are complicated and can take years to sort through. I will share just a few things I have learned from counselors and friends who are much more qualified than me to speak on such things. You will never heal from the mess of emotions that overwhelm you until you pull each one apart from the whole, face it, and sort through it. When confusion rears its ugly head from time to time in my relationship with my wife, she will ask me to talk to someone who is qualified and can help me sort through my emotions. Then my counselor and I sort things out one by one. Why the anger today? The regret? What fueled this frustration? Each one must be processed. You must face what you want healing from. Emotions that come from loving an addict are complex, and escaping them is the easier route. But it's not the long-term play. When you face them with someone who can handle them, you can find true healing.

> You will never heal from the mess of emotions that overwhelm you until you pull each one apart from the whole, face it, and sort through it.

I truly believe my mom was doing the best she knew how. And I believe the same about the Chris who tried to help her. I believe if she knew better, she would have done better. She just didn't know. She didn't have the tools or access to the same things I do today. Going to counseling or a rehab center wasn't an option in her world. Getting an accountability partner would never have crossed her mind as an option. Finding people to pray over her—nope. These things were not tools in her toolbox like they would be in mine if I faced her problems today. And the Chris who stepped in to help her, the little boy who gave her his extra work money, the one who told her how mad he was at her for the choices she was making . . . he was doing the best he knew how to as well. He did not have the emotional, physical, or spiritual tools he has today.

Release the guilt and shame that say you could have done better or you should have done better. I want to bet that you were doing the best you could with what you knew at the time. You have a God who remembers that you are human. He knows the limitations you are working with. Psalm 103:14 says, "For he knows how weak we are; he remembers we are only dust" (NLT). You should remember that about yourself as well.

15

Unfair Blame

Mom survived the seizure episode that day. She was taken to the hospital and after a few days was released and sent home. Joel stayed with us for about a week, but after that the guilt got to him as well. He begged us to let him go back and stay with Mom because she needed him and relied on him. We relented, and Joel returned to that very dark place. When I dropped him off at her house, my mom told me she had found a job as a waitress and was starting that evening. I thought this was a step in the right direction. Maybe she had finally learned a lesson. I was tentatively hopeful that things might work out after all.

I should have known better. Things didn't work out. Not even close. When Holly and I had been married for about two months, and about a month after Mom's major seizure scare, I came home from baseball practice to have a quick bite to eat before I had to head to work. While Holly fixed the food, I set up the ironing board and decided to turn on the TV to catch up on the five o'clock news while I pressed my white Oxford shirt.

The next thing I knew, the news anchor was talking about a wreck that had happened on a street near our apartment. She said the road had been shut down and advised taking an alternate route. I began to feel stress creeping up my chest because that was my route to work, and now I was going to really have to hurry to make it on time. I asked Holly if she could throw my dinner in a container because I was going to have to take it to go. I hustled to finish ironing my shirt, but as I did, I continued listening to the news story. The anchor said both parties were airlifted to the hospital. The woman at fault was intoxicated, and she was driving a brown 1979 Dodge Diplomat.

I didn't even have to look up at the screen. I knew it was my mom.

My mom had made the local news for drunk driving and had possibly just killed someone. My stomach sank. I began to feel physically sick. The room was spinning, and panic was coming fast. Was Joel with her? Would the people she hit die? Would she go to jail? Was she alive still? Was I hoping this was the end for her, or was I hoping she would survive this and go to jail? I didn't know. I didn't know which one I was hoping for.

It had been only three months since my dad had died, and I wasn't ready to deal with this. Holly walked into the living room to hand me a Tupperware container with my dinner. The second she saw the screen her jaw dropped. "Chris, isn't that your mom's car?" Oh no, even though we were married, I was not ready for Holly to know how dark things could be in my world. I shared with her often, but always only as much as I thought a girl from a great family and upbringing could handle at one time. She didn't know the full scope of Mom's struggle with addiction. She had never seen her have a seizure or start drinking first thing in the morning. She never would have guessed that my mom would chance driving drunk. She didn't know she already had two other DUIs. And yet, her totaled car was on the evening news as Holly watched in complete shock and horror.

I didn't have time to explain more to Holly or worry how all this was affecting her. We had to get to the hospital to find out if Joel was okay. Holly drove, and while I didn't say a word on the way, I was freaking out inside. My mom might have simultaneously killed my brother and others. And if I'm being completely honest, I was angry that she might have just ruined this new life I was building, and I was afraid of what was waiting for me at the other end of this drive.

Once the receptionist met us and sorted out who we were through our half sentences and panic, she was able to relieve my greatest fear by assuring me that my brother had not been in the car. Tears of relief flooded me. For privacy reasons, she could not tell me how the people Mom had hit were doing, but she did tell me that Mom was alive. She pointed us to a waiting room and let us know that the doctor would be in shortly to give us an update on Mom.

Moments later, the doctor arrived looking frustrated and tired. Over the years, I have learned that this is the common look families of addicts receive from hospital employees. I get it, you have given your life to help others, and then you have days when you must give your time away from your family to help those who can't even help themselves and in worst cases like this even harm others. There is very little empathy for those whose addictions land them in the hospital. He told us that Mom was going to be okay. We found out a couple of days later through a lawsuit that was being filed against Mom that the people in the other car had survived as well. Relief and anger washed over me at the same time.

Relief flooded me that no one had died or was facing life-long issues, but so much anger was rising in me toward my mom—an anger so intense it actually scared me. Holly and I were both working overtime so we could pay for a roof over our heads. We were newlyweds, and we barely saw each other with school, baseball, and extra shifts at work. Mom had a place to live, a place she didn't have to do special favors for, and yet here she was still doing stupid things. I had had enough. I went to the hospital staff and asked if I could speak to a social worker. I told the social worker *everything* and asked what Holly and I could do to keep Joel for good. I wanted custody of my brother, and I wanted my mom to go somewhere people wouldn't let her drink. Whatever the social worker needed to do to make those things happen, I wanted her to do. She asked if I had any older relatives who were close enough for us to call. I told her the truth. There was no one we were close enough with at the time. She was going to have to do this with me.

That day, two months after my wedding day, thirteen-year-old Joel moved in with Holly and me. We were nineteen and twenty-two at the time. And Mom? Well, I used the Florida Baker Act, which allowed me to put her in a mental health treatment center for a few days. All of this was against her wishes, of course. I think that was the straw that broke our relationship. Things had switched, and now I was the one in charge. She was the one being cared for and not often the way she wanted to be cared for. The next few years were filled with a mix of grace for my mom and her addiction, guilt for not being there enough for her, and absolute frustration that she kept relapsing again and again.

Joel spent the next few years in his own cycle of relief from not having to deal with Mom, her addiction, and her seizures and guilt for not being there to take care of her. He would live with us for a while, and then the guilt would overwhelm him, and he'd ask to go back to help Mom (who had found a boyfriend and moved to a different state). He'd stay with her until things became unbearable, and then he'd find his way back to us.

It was a mess. A hard way to navigate the teen years for Joel and a hard way to start a marriage for Holly and me. But we all made it. Together, Holly and I (with the help of her parents) got Joel through those middle school and high school years, we paid the rent, and Holly and I both got our degrees. Even my mom and I started to slowly repair our relationship once Joel was grown and she didn't feel as if I was stealing him from her. But things changed after that night in the hospital. Something was always different between us. I think for the first time my mom realized that I was determined not to live the same life she was living . . . nor would I let my brother live it. I think that broke her a little. She wavered just as much in her feelings toward me as I did toward her. She would send Christmas gifts in the mail and gush over her love for me, and then only a month later, I would receive an email that spewed her hate and embarrassment that I was her child. Dysfunction is just a constant breaking back and forth, isn't it? You break me; I break you. Over and over that cycle spins like a CD playing on repeat until there is nothing left of either of you.

My mom would often blame and resent me for my "interference" in her life. It's a tough pill to swallow when your oldest child has to Baker Act you and force you into detox treatment. That is still hard to put down on paper today. My mind is racing right now remembering how quiet the room was as four nurses and doctors waited on me to decide what I wanted to do with her. They could not give me advice or counsel, so they just presented my options. Then I sat there in silence wondering what was best for her and for us . . . in the short term and the long term. I was trying to make the wisest decision I could before I felt like I had any wisdom at all.

> Dysfunction is just a constant breaking back and forth, isn't it? You break me; I break you.

I wish she had known how little desire I had to get involved in her life and how much I was looking forward to getting on with my own adult life. In my mind, my "interference" was not optional but absolutely necessary. As you can imagine, I felt this was unfair blame, and it often crippled and confused me. She would blame me for losing her job because of being forced into detox and then blame me for the chain reaction it caused of being late on bills and not being able to find another job. Through the confusion, I would start to blame myself, thinking I had done the wrong thing.

Maybe you find yourself in the middle of some unfair blame. The best advice I have received that has helped me the most throughout the years is so simple you may get a little mad at me. But if you give it some thought, you will realize that it is pretty thorough advice: focus on what you can control. There is nothing more frustrating and disempowering than focusing on what you can't control. This goes for all of life but especially for the blame game. From the stressed-out guy in traffic who thinks cutting you off when you are actually going fifteen miles per hour over the speed limit, to the nosy woman at the grocery store who thinks you have too many items in your cart for the ten-items-or-less lane, to the spouse who blames you for their countless affairs. Focusing on those motives, decisions, or perspectives is disempowering, and those are all things you can't control.

What we can control is trying to do the right thing at all times and letting God fight our battles for us. That's what we can control, and it's much more empowering. We have to realize that we are naturally control freaks; we think we can control other people's decisions and perspectives . . . but we can't. What we *can* control is our own decisions, perspectives, reactions, attitudes, and behaviors.

> Your past pain has present purpose.

What about *past* blame? Chris, do we really need to go there? Is there a need to dig up the past? You better believe it. Your past pain has present purpose, and you need to go to work to redeem it and give it purpose to help others and to glorify God. That process is what this whole book is about and the journey you agreed to in chapter 1. You got this. I promise your soul will thank you. Trust me. If you've ever been blamed for something significant in the past, I invite you not only to recall the blame but also to go back and mentally and emotionally relive it for the sole purpose of doing something redemptive with it, perhaps even leveraging it to help others experiencing a similar pain. I promise that the soul-deep rewards will far outweigh the torment of rolling back the clock on the event.

16

Choosing Community

A couple of years after the fallout from her DUI accident, Mom remarried. Her husband was a good man. When my mom was with him, I know she tried her best to keep her addiction in check. While I don't believe she stopped drinking, I think she did better with him than she had done in years. But she had put her body through the wringer for most of her life, and at the young age of fifty-four, Mom died from complications due to pneumonia. She refused to go to the hospital until it was too late. Refused probably because she knew she would not be able to drink or smoke if they admitted her. Finally, she got so bad that she went, and she was almost immediately intubated. Her body simply couldn't overcome sickness and withdrawal at the same time. Addiction had finally won.

In her last few years, my mom talked about the Lord and read her Bible often. While I believe that my mom was a Christian, I had to come face-to-face with the truth that she never found freedom from her addiction this side of heaven. This world is hard, harder on some than others, and sometimes addiction wins. And that's hard to accept. This world has not yet been fully redeemed, and despite how hard we pray, how much we believe God can heal, sometimes it doesn't come. Sometimes we must deal with the disappointment that our prayers were not answered in the way we had hoped they would be.

This world is hard, harder on some than others, and sometimes addiction wins. And that's hard to accept.

Just because my mom never found freedom certainly does not mean that she is not with Jesus. I wholeheartedly believe that when we know God, his Spirit resides in us, and because of that alone, we do have the power in us to overcome our strongholds and our addictions. But I also know that we all have a choice. And once addiction has hijacked the brain, it's not as simple a choice. That choice means withdrawals, it means facing the pain you've spent years trying to numb, and it means work. Hard, hard work. Some simply don't have the fight left in them to make that choice. We should all try to have grace for those who find themselves addicted with no fight left. I work toward being this kind of grace-filled person, but I am not naive. I know from firsthand experience that when you love someone who is an addict, it's complicated.

What I didn't know until my mom passed is that when you lose that loved one who has battled addiction, you are left with a confused mess in your own heart and mind. No one tells you that you will be flooded simultaneously with relief, grief, anger, and frustration. No one assures you that you are not a monster for those feelings of relief. Relief that the fighting is over, the panic of not knowing where they are for weeks at a time is over, the stomach-sinking feeling you get every time a number you don't recognize appears on your phone is over. All of it is finally over. And your heart is relieved. And in the very next breath, your heart grieves. Grieves that they are gone. Grieves that they never found freedom from their addiction. Grieves that you didn't do more, help more, say more life-giving things to them in their darkest moment. And then one more breath and the anger floods in. Why didn't they try harder? Why didn't they love me enough to quit? Why did they put us through so much useless pain for so long? Anger comes from feeling powerless as a child because you were trapped in a prison the addict placed you in. A prison of poverty, shame, frustration, guilt, anger, depression, and helplessness. As your heart rides the waves of each conflicting emotion, frustration swells above them all like the one wave that is surely going to put you under for good once it crashes over you. Frustration stems from the fact that family roles were flipped upside down on you at too young an age. You became the parent, and they became the child. This was a responsibility that was theirs to carry, and they dumped it on you when you did not have the emotional tools necessary to carry this heavy a weight. You were just a child. And now that you are grown, now that you know what it means to be an adult, to be a parent, that frustration fills the space on your shoulders where the family responsibility once sat.

Relief, grief, anger, and frustration . . . which emotion wins in your heart each day changes as often as the tide on the shore. And then there is one more emotion that puts your heart into the biggest tailspin of all. Your heart feels comparable to a child bodysurfing at the beach and that one *huge* wave you have been waiting on finally comes, but as it crests above your head, you realize, "Oh no. I underestimated this sucker." And then you go on the biggest "ride or die" of your life. You begin flipping under the water in every direction, you feel the sand filling up your trunks, the seaweed whipping through your hair, and all you are doing is trying to figure out if you should cry or laugh. You can't decide if this is the best thing ever or the final moment of your life. And after a few moments, you relax and just enjoy the ride, knowing that sand is removable, seaweed can be brushed out of hair, and a few bumps and bruises are worth the price of riding the wave.

That's the way it feels when love sweeps over you as you grieve. Love because you remember the good. Everyone else who didn't know the situation up close and personal will just remember the unfortunate and too-often-told story of another addict dying. But you intimately knew them. You knew *all* of them. You will remember the good times as well. You will remember how hard they fought to put a roof over your head. You will remember how they sacrificed in order to buy you a puppy. The inside jokes you had together. Love will whip you around when you remember their laugh—the genuine one that wasn't induced by happy pills, the real, soul-deep "I am satisfied with life right now" laugh.

I decided that while I did have a lot of conflicting emotions around my mom and the life I lived while I was with her, I was going to do the work to release those feelings and ride the wave of love that I felt when it came. I'll be honest, I don't feel this way every day, because I didn't feel loved every day by my mom. But I am okay with that now. My mom wasn't perfect, but she still stayed, and she loved me to the capacity that she had. She didn't love me as I know love today, but she loved me as much as she knew how. She loved me with the tools she was given in her life. She wasn't given many tools in her own childhood, and I choose to have grace for her because of that. Her love for me was mangled and twisted and immature, but it was what she knew, and I believe she was doing the best she could. I know that now. I honor her. It may seem unlikely to you, but my mom, with her addiction and all, still died one of my heroes. She stayed. And she stayed when I had no one else.

My mom's life was no different from the lives of most people who struggle with addiction. She let very few people into her life. Except for her husband in her last few years, she hid herself from people at all costs. She had no friends, no community when she passed. Her shame drove her to hide. To cover. In the end, she died feeling lonely, shamed, and forgotten. Rejected by society. That's not who she was. That's not who God created her to be, but that is how she died. Isolated with only her husband and two sons by her side. Prior to my marriage to Holly, this is how I lived a lot of my own life. It's what I knew. Keep it all hidden. Don't let anyone in. No one gets to see behind the door of your home or your soul. That is a space that is too dark, too shameful for people to peer into.

But after Holly and I married, she unknowingly began to pull me out of my isolation and into a life of community. Life with people was what Holly knew. And it wasn't just Holly, although it started with her. It was her family as well and the people God brought into our path as newlyweds. I began to learn that there are better ways to do this life than trying to muscle through in isolation. Slowly, God began to teach me that people can be trusted. They can know who you really are and still choose to love you. God began to rewrite a new normal in my life, a normal that brought healing to places addiction had deeply wounded.

Sunday lunch with my in-laws was a new normal. Holly had a great family. Her parents married when they were just out of high school, and they were still married when her dad died. They loved each other. They loved their kids. They worked regular jobs. Holly's parents lived in a two-story house in a middle-class neighborhood, but to me, it might as well have been a mansion. Every Sunday after church, her parents hosted Sunday lunch, and *everyone* in the family attended. Holly's parents, her four siblings, and everyone's spouse or significant other all showed up every single week. I kept thinking to myself, *Is this for real? Will they get grounded for not showing up? Do people really sit around the table and just chitchat about seemingly inconsequential things for hours on end, things that are funny, things that unfolded that week, or new opportunities they were chasing?* I couldn't keep up with the constant chatter. For years, I sat there quietly and wondered, *Who really lives like this?* I just sat in the corner of this massive crowd each week waiting for the other shoe to drop in some way. Don't get me wrong. They had their share of problems, but what made their family special was that they shared their problems together. And they seemed to love it that way.

It was all slightly overwhelming to me. I remember one evening after we had attended a couple of these Sunday lunches as a married couple, Holly said, "Hey. When we go

> I began to learn that there are better ways to do this life than trying to muscle through in isolation. Slowly, God began to teach me that people can be trusted.

to Sunday lunch and you are the first one in the food line, can you look at the amount of meat available and then divide by how many people are there and start with that size of a serving?" I had no idea I was doing it, but I would just pile and pile my food on and never once consider that the women in the back of the line would end up eating vegetarian that day. I realized then I still had a lot of poverty mindset lingering in me, and Holly was picking up on it. That was another new normal God was creating. I wouldn't starve. Empty stomachs were a thing of the past. Silent dinners in separate rooms were no more. God is a God of enough.

In addition to Sunday lunches, Holly's family hosted a birthday dinner for each person on their birthday. When I had my birthday for the first time as a part of this family, they all circled up in her parents' living room, and then each person took a turn not only handing me a gift but also saying something they admired or appreciated about me. They called it "affirmations." *What the what?!?* I thought. *Surely I'm in a twilight zone, and the world is going to blow up in a matter of seconds. This cannot be real life.* I'm not going to lie. This freaked me out a little at first, but it also was something so beautiful that I had never experienced before. My isolated, thirsty soul was soaking it up, and slowly but surely God was teaching me that life with people is so much more meaningful than life alone. I felt like a toddler learning about this new world in front of me with each and every step. Everything felt new. Everything felt different. I was like a little boy in a man's body with eyes full of wonder.

I was talking to Holly's mom recently over a bowl of pinto beans and ham. As we ate, I asked her, "You guys built such a beautiful family. You did so much right and protected your kids from so much dark in this world. Why in a million years did you let Holly marry me? You had to have known I was a disaster."

What she said blew me away. Her cousin Troy was a pastor and the officiant at our wedding. When he agreed to marry us, Troy called my mother-in-law and said that he wanted to ask her some questions about Holly and me. She said he's the one who helped her fully support our marriage and find peace with the decision Holly was making. She explained that Troy asked about Holly, and she told him how much Holly loved the Lord and how much her family supported her and trusted her decision-making. She assured him that she knew no matter what Holly faced in life, she had a strong support system. She went on to tell me, "I told Troy that I knew without a doubt that Holly loved you and you loved her." But then Troy said, "Tell me a little about Chris." My mother-in-law said, "Well, Chris, well . . . Chris is not at all what a mom would pray for her daughter. He's quite the opposite. Don't get me wrong. He seems to be a great guy, but his life has been surrounded by instability, addiction, and poverty. His father is absent, and from what I can tell, Chris is doing most of the providing and parenting for his younger brother. I would be lying if I didn't admit that I am a little nervous about the whole thing."

But Troy's response changed her thinking. He said, "Becky, you are looking at this only from Holly's side. You are her mother; you love her so much, and you want the best for her. But God feels the same way about Chris. He isn't just looking at this marriage from Holly's side; he is looking at it from Chris's side as well. Holly may be God's gift to heal some of what he's been through. To help carry the weight with him. To encourage him when it seems too much to bear. Maybe God is asking you to give Holly to Chris because of his love for Chris. Would you be okay with that?" Not only was she okay with it, but she sacrificed deeply for my healing, and not just mine but Joel's as well.

When Holly and I first married, we tag-teamed college. Holly worked sixty to seventy hours a week until I graduated, and then I went to work sixty to seventy hours a week to put her through nursing school. Not only were we both trying to finish our degrees, but we were also learning to parent a teenager, since Joel moved in with us not long after we married. It wasn't long before we realized that even though we dearly loved each other, we needed mentors and we needed help if we were going to do this for the long haul. Joel's life hadn't been easy, and the effects of it made things a little more challenging than what one would encounter when parenting a teen who hadn't been through the things he had. There were days when Joel's emotional and schooling needs became too overwhelming for us. Soon Holly's parents opened up their home to Joel for a couple of weeks at a time so that Holly and I had time alone as newlyweds to focus on our marriage and learn how to make a way in this world together. We were less than a year into this marriage and in-law thing, and this couple, who was facing a devastating diagnosis with my father-in-law, who had an uncertain future to say the least, extended their arms, their wallets, and their hearts to my brother. I never knew anyone to sacrifice like this for someone they barely knew without some kind of personal payoff. Joel spent time with Holly's parents, and slowly God began to teach him what a healthy family looked like.

Joel's normal was being changed just like mine was. Things that had been broken for so long began to heal as he felt included in the life of a healthy family. His hopes and dreams started to grow, and he began to see a future for himself that just a few months earlier seemed so out of reach for people like us. He too was learning that life with people is better than life alone.

During this time, I was working my first salary job as a teacher and athletic director at a local Christian school, and as soon as the school got wind of just a part of my story, they gave my brother a full scholarship to attend the high school. He was surrounded by Christian teachers who loved him for who he was. They were graceful with the gaps he had because of the childhood he had endured. They were kind and, most of all, patient with Joel. Joel met Jesus at that school. In a matter of months, his schooling was paid for, he had a stable home to live in, and people at our school and church and in my newfound family were rallying around us with love and support like I had never known before. I didn't know it at the time, but what I was experiencing was biblical community. This is what Paul meant when he said, "Carry each other's burdens" (Gal. 6:2). They were carrying this weight with me, and for once, the overwhelming burden of dysfunction, addiction, and poverty didn't seem quite so heavy. Life with people was tearing down the prison walls that addiction and shame had built around my heart. The walls that didn't let anyone in and at the same time held me captive. Good people, God's people, saw how much healing and acceptance we needed, and they stepped up to the plate. They simply showed up and offered what they had to give. Slowly, I began to realize that life in community was healing what life in isolation had destroyed. Brick by brick, life in community tore down the walls of my isolating prison.

Maybe you too are in a place where you find yourself facing so many conflicting emotions because of the role addiction has played in the life of someone you love or maybe in your own life. Like I said at the beginning of this book, I am not a licensed counselor or therapist, but I do know that addiction shames us into isolation. In isolation, all the dark things grow: our shame, our loneliness, our depression, and our own addictions or coping mechanisms. The only way to fight this is to come out of isolation and choose to live in community with others.

Find a strong community that can support you as you walk through this life. Don't do life alone. Especially if you love someone who struggles with addiction or you are still carrying the wounds from what addiction did to you as a child, you need others. This is too much for you to carry by yourself, and God doesn't want you to carry all those wounds on your own. He has a community of people waiting to help you carry the load. You don't have to be the sole hero. Let others in. You can do this slowly, but take a step toward cracking open the door of your soul to others. There is healing in simply letting others know the weight on your shoulders and the pain in your past. God can use good people to heal the wounds caused by addiction in your life.

17

The Power of Focus

Holly's dad passed away a few years into our marriage. We were at her parents' house, and he collapsed in the bathroom. Holly was fresh out of nursing school, so naturally, she was the one who did CPR on her father on the bathroom floor. He was her hero, and he was also the first patient she ever lost. Despite all her efforts and the "Jesus, help us!" cries she sent out between breaths, she couldn't save him.

Her family grieved hard after he died. He was so loved. I knew then that I wanted a family like this. A family that loves together, grieves together, and carries each other through hard times. But I had no idea how to build such a family. I wondered, *How do I make this part of my story?* I knew what I wanted, but I had no idea how to get there.

Here we were, just a few years into our marriage, and Holly and I had both buried our fathers. I remember sitting at our kitchen table one day feeling overwhelmed. I was watching Holly and her family grieve, and I was grieving myself, since her father was the only picture of a true father I had ever known. I was also looking for a new job, so the pressure of that was mounting at the same time.

Then I remembered Psalm 68:5–6: "Father to the fatherless, defender of widows—this is God, whose dwelling is holy. God places the lonely in families" (NLT). I felt God whisper into my soul, "I know you are fatherless. I know that in most ways you've always been fatherless. Holly also is now fatherless. I see both of you and know your needs. I see her grief. I know your longings for a father to help you make your way in this world. I will be what you and Holly need from an earthly father."

Almost instantly, I felt this deep settling in me. I knew God was telling me, "You know how a dad will pull strings to help his child have opportunities? You know how a dad gives his child good things? How he bails him out with money when he needs it and treats him to some steak and potatoes after a hard workout? I know a good dad does those things. Chris, I will be that dad to you and Holly. You have no idea the strings I'm pulling for you. You have no idea the good things and the food I want to lavish on you guys. [I was a young man, and food was the number one way to my heart. Okay, it still is.] Chris, you will be a provider. You will be a protector. I will step in and love you just as anyone else's well-connected father would for them. Except I'm God, and I have all the connections and unlimited resources. I am personally taking you and Holly under my wing." In that moment at that yard sale–purchased

> I knew then that I wanted a family like this. A family that loves together, grieves together, and carries each other through hard times.

kitchen table, I felt the same way I did when I saw that one-thousand-dollar check my dad wrote to my mom: I am going to be okay. I have a rich Dad, and he lives nearby.

And God did take care of us just as a well-connected, rich earthly father would take care of his child. An opportunity I never dreamed of fell in my lap just a few weeks later. I was not qualified for the job, and yet there I was sitting in a chair I shouldn't have been sitting in. And then a few years later, another job I was not qualified for came knocking on my door, and then another and another. With every job, I looked at the nameplate on the door and shook my head in disbelief. Today, I can tell you that I have not worked one job in which I went into the interview qualified for the position. In fact, once a recruiter called me and asked if I would be interested in interviewing for a speaking position that operated on a national level. Up until this point in my career, I rarely spoke. So naturally, it took a couple of phone calls from this recruiter for me to believe that he wasn't pulling my leg. But since I try hard to operate under the "say yes" mentality when it comes to opportunity, I decided to go through with the interview process.

I will never forget meeting with the board of this nationally known company. The only question I remember them asking was this: "Chris, tell us why we should hire you when we have 250 applicants, most of whom have already published books or have a popular blog?" I sat there as someone who at that point had only ever written things of 140 characters or less and who could easily recall being pulled off the stage the first time I tried to do announcements for a church because I was so bad. I looked them straight in the eye and said, "I have no idea why you would choose me over them. I think you might be better off hiring one of them." I was offered the position before I left their boardroom that day. The *only* way I can explain it is . . . I have a really good Dad. He is a Father to the fatherless.

Maybe you are like Holly and me and you no longer have a father here on earth. Or maybe he is physically still alive but opted out of being a present father long ago. You, my friend, have access to the same Father who has taken me under his wing. He will do the same for you. Listen to me: Maybe you have been dealt a terrible hand. Your hand cannot affect your life for bad nearly as much as your Father can affect it for good. You have a rich Father who lives nearby. A Father who is rich in the amount of love he has for you. Rich in the resources he wants to lavish on you. He isn't mad at you. He isn't lording punishment over you. He is rich in grace toward you, and even if you caused the storm you are currently in, he will calm it. He will use your current storm to help you. To make things in your life beautiful again. Financially, emotionally, physically, you are going to make it through the deepest valleys in your life because you too have access to the Father.

> He is rich in grace toward you, and even if you caused the storm you are currently in, he will calm it.

Okay, Chris, that sounds good, but how do I do this? How do I shift my focus from the pain of what I am going through to the access I have been given by my heavenly Father? First and foremost, train your mind to focus on who your Father is. I know this can be easier said than done, so let me show you a little trick I use to shift my focus from the situation in front of me to the God who fathers me.

Take a piece of paper and fold it lengthwise. On one side, write down what you are worried about or what's causing you stress at the moment. Sometimes my mind gets the best of me, and I will literally write down the worst-case scenario about the situation I am facing. Line by line, write these things down. All of them. The simple things stressing you as well as the big things. Just get them down on paper. Once you have completed this, open the page, and line by line write down what you know is true about your heavenly Father. And if all of this is new to you, research the promises of God. You may need to borrow the faith of others until you have developed faith of your own.

Here's how this works.

Stressor: Finding a job

I am not qualified for the job I am chasing.	My God could find me a job with his eyes closed, and he is with me. He will equip me. In a moment, God can make up for lost time. In a moment, he can qualify me to do this work. First Samuel 10:9–10 says, "As Saul turned to leave Samuel, God changed Saul's heart, and all these signs were fulfilled that day. . . . The Spirit of God came powerfully upon him, and he joined in their prophesying."
The people I interview with won't like me.	My God who is on my side controls how they will perceive me. He controls perceptions. Proverbs 21:1 says, "The king's heart is like a stream of water directed by the LORD; he guides it wherever he pleases" (NLT).
I won't make enough to provide for Holly and me.	I will get a paycheck from this job, but my provision and needs will be met by my heavenly Father. He favors me. Our needs are a simple fix to him. He will provide. Psalm 50:10 says, "For every animal of the forest is mine, and the cattle on a thousand hills." Philippians 4:19 says, "And my God will meet all your needs according to the riches of his glory in Christ Jesus."

Try it. Pray out loud everything you wrote down that you know is true about your Father. Go ahead, take a moment to do it. I promise you will feel better. Nothing will change about what you are facing, but when you take the time to reassure yourself of who your Father is and focus on him more than your circumstances, your heart will begin to calm.

18

A Call to Restoration

I swung through the kitchen, grabbed a cold LimonCello LaCroix, and collapsed in one of the white rocking chairs on the front porch of our two-hundred-year-old farmhouse. We purchased this old, dilapidated hobby farm out in the country four years ago. And I spent today, my day off, doing what I love: restoring another part of this old farm.

Today, I worked on our fencing, making sure our horses and dogs could not venture off the property and find themselves in danger on the train tracks behind us or the road in front of us. As I sat there with sweat still rolling down my back and stinging my eyes, I just stared blankly at the last few minutes of the Tennessee sun setting. I enjoyed the view as mindlessly as possible for a few minutes. There is something healing in just taking in nature without having to think.

I continued to sit there long after the sunset, and my mind began to get its second wind. It trailed down one path to another, from the kids and who was headed in what direction tonight, to the needs of the church that I work for, to whether or not Holly and I finished that Netflix documentary before falling asleep last night. Up one trail and down another it went for several minutes. I found myself just thanking God for the life he has given me, for what he has restored in me. As I sat there and rocked as dusk swept over me and the crickets began their nightly chirping, I realized that my hobby of restoring this old farm meant so much more than fixing broken fences.

> I found myself just thanking God for the life he has given me, for what he has restored in me.

When Holly and I bought this farm, it had been abandoned for several years. The fact that the two-hundred-year-old home was being sold "as is" contributed to very few interested buyers. Everything that could be wrong with an abandoned place was wrong with this place. The outside was overrun with moles, and ladybugs and critters lived in every barn and shed. When we walked the property for the first time with our buying agent, we commented that it sounded like the Rain Forest Cafe outside. We have now learned that when the outside sounds this way, it is charming to walk through but difficult to live in. All those sounds are families upon families of nonhuman beings whose space you are invading. They don't appreciate your presence. And they aren't respectful to give you your space and stay on the outside of the four walls of your home. Once we signed on the dotted line, we quickly learned that the inside was inhabited with its fair share of stinkbugs, wasps, mice, and snakes as well. Holly was super-excited about sharing our living space with slithering friends. Leaks in pipes and cracks in the walls and floors were everywhere.

The first time Holly took a shower in the house, the shower literally fell through the ceiling and into the dining room. This place was a disaster, and it didn't take long for us to realize why no locals had wanted to touch it with a ten-foot pole.

The farm was run down, forgotten, and abandoned. The locals had given up on it. We saw this scenario in front of us when we looked at the property the first time. Just like everyone else, we didn't think it was worth the money. The work was too much and would probably bankrupt us. There was no guarantee that the house could be salvaged. But as we walked the thirty acres, something began to come alive in us. As we tentatively ventured through one run-down barn after another, we began to see the beauty of what could be.

The main home was a log cabin. Each piece of that home had been built by someone who had chopped and chopped and chopped. Whose sweat had rolled down his back while his mind had dreamed of his family arriving at sunset to peek at the progress he had made on their home that day. From sunup to sundown for months at a time, hands blistered and bleeding, some father had kept chopping to create a haven for those he loved. As we toured the small home, I ran my hand along those walls and could feel every single mark of the axe on each log. A father had put a lot of love and labor into this home. And two hundred years later, the work of his hands and the labor of his love was still standing. As we ventured through the small log cabin, we began to visualize what this run-down place could be again. We began to forget about all the damage and the dollars it would cost to restore, and we began to see the potential. There was so much uniqueness about a home like this. There was so much history. Two hundred years of Christmases held in the front room. Walls that existed before indoor plumbing and electricity existed. If walls could talk, these would be the ones I would want to hear from.

It wasn't long before we began to get excited at the possibility of restoring something everyone else had given up on. Something in us wanted to show the city that this eyesore could be beautiful again. It deserved to be beautiful again. This property was beat up and run down, yes, but it wasn't dead. It wasn't over.

That was four years ago, and as I worked on my 765th restoration project on this farm today, I realized that the process of repairing this old place and making it into something beautiful isn't just a fun Joanna Gaines restoration project. It's a picture of my life. I too was forgotten. I was abandoned, and rejection consumed me. I sat in the ruins of my own pain.

But God.

But God decided that I was worth fighting for. Dying for. I was a major renovation project. One most people would pass up, never look twice at, and if they did, they would surely decide they'd bankrupt themselves on me. I was not worth the effort. I would cost more than I could ever benefit. But God is not a God who considers his return on investment when he loves. He just loves, because to him, I am worthy. Worthy to be loved. Worthy to be repaired and restored. Worthy of fighting for the beauty that resides under all the ruins. I saw ruins; he saw beauty. I saw a kid whose father never paid attention to him until it was too late, but he saw a man he traded his Son's life for. He gave his most precious possession to have me. He wanted me. He pursued me. He came along and began to build something beautiful from my ruins. He didn't throw me out and start over with someone shiny and new. Someone who had a prettier repertoire to start with. God chose me just as I was—banged up and bruised—and began to build from what was. He bought me *as is*. And slowly but surely, he is transforming me into something beautiful. As I process one painful part of my story after another with God, he shows me the beauty that can be found in it. He is making my story into something beautiful. He is not deleting parts of my past; he is transforming them.

And as I sat on that porch, I solidified something in my heart. My newfound hobby of repairing fences, rebuilding barns, and restoring the logs of this weathered home is a reflection of not only what has been done in me but also what I want to give my life to. I want to be a part of the repair process of people's lives. I want to show up when everyone else walks out. I want to be a restorer. Not of farms but of hearts.

Then you will be known as a rebuilder of walls and a restorer of homes. (Isa. 58:12 NLT)

Afterword

Dear reader, your ruins are worthy of being restored. Your past pain is worthy of being cultivated into present purpose. I don't care who has given up on you. I want you to know that I haven't . . . and neither has your heavenly Father. He makes *all* things beautiful. And that, my friend, includes your soul and your past. Past pain transformed into present purpose is your right in your Father's kingdom.

Please know that I have been praying for you for over a year and will continue to pray that God will bless you and everything you put your hand to. May your relationships thrive. May your schoolwork excel. May your career take off. May your faith be strengthened. May your soul's thirst be quenched.

If you have read this book and as a result are curious about what a relationship with Jesus could look like in your life, please email me chris@thewellcolumbia.org. I would be honored to personally walk you through the most important decision you will ever make in your life.

Let's all stay connected, my friends. Please feel free to reach out anytime at @chrisbrownonair on all social media platforms. And you can follow along with the church we just launched last year (The Well) at thewellcolumbia.org to see what we've been up to.

Much love,
Chris Brown

About the Author

Chris Brown is a highly sought-after pastor, speaker, and church leadership expert. Chris has over twenty years of ministry and financial experience. He worked alongside Dave Ramsey for years as a nationally syndicated radio host for *Life, Money, and Hope.* and has been featured on national media outlets such as *Fox & Friends.* But most importantly, he passionately loves Jesus.

Chris wakes up each morning with one thing on his mind, and that's impact. Chris wants to make a long-lasting difference in as many people's lives as possible. Chris's professional career has included Christian school teaching, real estate, church consulting, leadership coaching, and leading at the highest level at incredibly successful churches like Elevation Church in Charlotte, North Carolina; Potential Church in Cooper City, Florida; and Crosspoint Church in Nashville, Tennessee.

In 2021, Chris and his wife, Holly, launched a church called The Well in Columbia, Tennessee, with the same restoration heartbeat that radiates from the pages of this book.

Chris and Holly have been married for over twenty years and have a thriving marriage that is anchored in their faith and fueled by their partnership in ministry. Chris and Holly traded in city life for farm life in Columbia, Tennessee, with their three children.

Get to Know Chris

Head to **chrisbrownonair.com** to learn more about Chris, watch his messages, read his blog, or get in touch!

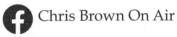 Chris Brown On Air

 ChrisBrownOnAir

 ChrisBrownOnAir